JOE WARD MUNROW

Joe Ward Munrow is an award-winning playwright from Deptford, South London, who has been based in Liverpool for over twenty years.

His previous plays includes *Screaming Heart* (winner of the Mercury Weinberger playwriting award), *Blue* (The Gate, London, and Royal Welsh College of Music and Drama), *The Busker* (BBC Radio 4), *Hercules and Phoebe* (National Theatre 'Let's Play' Tour), *Dogs* (Liverpool Playhouse Studio), *The Laundry* (Brockley Jack Studio Theatre) and *Held* (Liverpool Playhouse Studio).

In 2022 Joe founded the theatre company New Step with writer and director Nathan Powell. New Step makes world-class theatre that is surprising, joyous and original. New Step shows are performed in professional theatres and are then taken on the road to communities. The shows are performed in whichever space suits that community best – it could be a youth centre, a warehouse, a boxing gym… anywhere.
(www.newsteptheatre.com)

Joe has previously led playwriting groups at the Liverpool Everyman, the Manchester Royal Exchange and the Royal Court, London. He is a lecturer in Scriptwriting at Manchester Metropolitan University.

Other Titles in this Series

Samuel Bailey
SHOOK
SORRY, YOU'RE NOT A WINNER

Mike Bartlett
THE 47TH
ALBION
BULL
GAME
AN INTERVENTION
KING CHARLES III
MRS DELGADO
SCANDALTOWN
SNOWFLAKE
VASSA *after* Gorky
WILD

Jez Butterworth
THE FERRYMAN
THE HILLS OF CALIFORNIA
JERUSALEM
JEZ BUTTERWORTH PLAYS: ONE
JEZ BUTTERWORTH PLAYS: TWO
MOJO
THE NIGHT HERON
PARLOUR SONG
THE RIVER
THE WINTERLING

Caryl Churchill
BLUE HEART
CHURCHILL PLAYS: THREE
CHURCHILL PLAYS: FOUR
CHURCHILL PLAYS: FIVE
CHURCHILL: SHORTS
CLOUD NINE
DING DONG THE WICKED
A DREAM PLAY *after* Strindberg
DRUNK ENOUGH TO SAY I LOVE YOU?
ESCAPED ALONE
FAR AWAY
GLASS. KILL. BLUEBEARD'S FRIENDS. IMP.
HERE WE GO
HOTEL
ICECREAM
LIGHT SHINING IN BUCKINGHAMSHIRE
LOVE AND INFORMATION
MAD FOREST
A NUMBER
PIGS AND DOGS
SEVEN JEWISH CHILDREN
THE SKRIKER
THIS IS A CHAIR
THYESTES *after* Seneca
TRAPS
WHAT IF IF ONLY

Dave Harris
TAMBO & BONES

Rhianna Ilube
SAMUEL TAKES A BREAK… IN MALE DUNGEON NO. 5 AFTER A LONG BUT GENERALLY SUCCESSFUL DAY OF TOURS

Branden Jacobs-Jenkins
APPROPRIATE
THE COMEUPPANCE
GLORIA
AN OCTOROON

Lucy Kirkwood
BEAUTY AND THE BEAST
 with Katie Mitchell
BLOODY WIMMIN
THE CHILDREN
CHIMERICA
HEDDA *after* Ibsen
THE HUMAN BODY
IT FELT EMPTY WHEN THE HEART WENT AT FIRST BUT IT IS ALRIGHT NOW
LUCY KIRKWOOD PLAYS: ONE
MOSQUITOES
NSFW
RAPTURE
TINDERBOX
THE WELKIN

Suzie Miller
PRIMA FACIE

Winsome Pinnock
LEAVE TAKING
ROCKETS AND BLUE LIGHTS
TAKEN
TITUBA

Sophie Swithinbank
BACON

Jack Thorne
2ND MAY 1997
AFTER LIFE
BUNNY
BURYING YOUR BROTHER IN THE PAVEMENT
A CHRISTMAS CAROL *after* Dickens
THE END OF HISTORY…
HOPE
JACK THORNE PLAYS: ONE
JUNKYARD
LET THE RIGHT ONE IN
 after John Ajvide Lindqvist
THE MOTIVE AND THE CUE
MYDIDAE
THE SOLID LIFE OF SUGAR WATER
STACY & FANNY AND FAGGOT
WHEN WINSTON WENT TO WAR WITH THE WIRELESS
WHEN YOU CURE ME
WOYZECK *after* Büchner

debbie tucker green
BORN BAD
DEBBIE TUCKER GREEN PLAYS: ONE
DIRTY BUTTERFLY
EAR FOR EYE
HANG
NUT
A PROFOUNDLY AFFECTIONATE, PASSIONATE DEVOTION TO SOMEONE (– *NOUN*)
RANDOM
STONING MARY
TRADE & GENERATIONS
TRUTH AND RECONCILIATION

Phoebe Waller-Bridge
FLEABAG

Joe Ward Munrow
BLUE

Joe Ward Munrow

THE LEGEND OF NED LUDD

NICK HERN BOOKS
London
www.nickhernbooks.co.uk

A Nick Hern Book

The Legend of Ned Ludd first published as a paperback original in Great Britain in 2024 by Nick Hern Books Limited, The Glasshouse, 49a Goldhawk Road, London W12 8QP

The Legend of Ned Ludd © 2024 Joe Ward Munrow

Joe Ward Munrow has asserted his right to be identified as the author of this work

Cover image: © iStock.com/ibusca

Designed and typeset by Nick Hern Books, London
Printed in Great Britain by Mimeo Ltd, Huntingdon, Cambridgeshire PE29 6XX

A CIP catalogue record for this book is available from the British Library

ISBN   978 1 83904 320 8

CAUTION   All rights whatsoever in this play are strictly reserved. Requests to reproduce the text in whole or in part should be addressed to the publisher.

Amateur Performing Rights   Applications for performance, including readings and excerpts, by amateurs in the English language throughout the world should be addressed to the Performing Rights Manager, Nick Hern Books, The Glasshouse, 49a Goldhawk Road, London W12 8QP, *tel* +44 (0)20 8749 4953, *email* rights@nickhernbooks.co.uk, except as follows:

Australia: ORiGiN Theatrical, *email* enquiries@originmusic.com.au, *web* www.origintheatrical.com.au

New Zealand: Play Bureau, 20 Rua Street, Mangapapa, Gisborne, 4010, *tel* +64 21 258 3998, *email* info@playbureau.com

USA and Canada: Casarotto Ramsay and Associates Ltd, see details below

Professional Performing Rights   Applications for performance by professionals in any medium and in any language throughout the world (including by stock companies in the USA and Canada) should be addressed to Casarotto Ramsay and Associates Ltd, *email* rights@casarotto.co.uk, www.casarotto.co.uk

No performance of any kind may be given unless a licence has been obtained. Applications should be made before rehearsals begin. Publication of this play does not necessarily indicate its availability for amateur performance.

www.nickhernbooks.co.uk/environmental-policy

The Legend of Ned Ludd was first performed at the Liverpool Everyman on 20 April 2024, with the following cast:

B	Reuben Johnson
A	Menyee Lai
C	Shaun Mason
Recorded Translations	Neelima Samaiya & Manuel Mouchipku
Director	Jude Christian
Set and Costume Designer	Hazel Low
Lighting Designer	Laura Howard
Sound Designer	Kieran Lucas
Costume Supervisor	Shellby Hamer
Voice Coach	Elspeth Morrison
Producer	Michelle Cailleux
Production Manager	Dan Franklin
Company Manager	Sarah Lewis
Stage Manager	Kate Eccles
Deputy Stage Manager	Roxanne Vella
Assistant Stage Manager	Kaila Sharples
Book Cover	Beth Lewis
Assistant Production Manager	Diego Gutiérrez Córdoba
Assistant Producer	Zoe Walker
LX Plotter	Jack Coleman
LX Operator	Jack Wood
Sound & AV Programmer	Ian Davies
Sound & AV Operators	Roxanne Vella & Kaila Sharples
Automation	Mike Cantley
Stage Crew	Jack Higham
Set Construction	RT Scenic
Wardrobe Maintenance	Eleanor Ager-Cantley
Captioned Performance	Steph Carter

Acknowledgements

This play took a very long time to write and the amount of people who helped get it over the line is huge.

My massive thanks go to Kevin Binfield, without whose book, *The Writings of the Luddites*, I wouldn't have been able to write the play.

Thanks also to: the brilliant writers, dramaturgs and directors who gave notes and helped hone the script. Jay Miller, Ashleigh Wheeler, Craig Gilbert, Ellie Horne, Lucy Morrison, Jane Fallowfield, Dan Hutton, Mark Ravenhill, Andy Routledge, Frank Peschier, Jen Tan, Tommo Fowler, and especially Jude Christian.

The amazing actors and makers who helped me in and out of the rehearsal room – Yusra Warsama, Joshua Higgott, Selma Brook, Simon Scardifield, Kirsty Ryder, Helen Carter, Reuben Johnson, Menyee Lai, Shaun Mason and especially Amaka Okafor and Thanh Le Dang.

The translators who helped me realise the global scope of the play – Stevie Duong, Joe Mak, Alena Baimukhametova, Julia Munrow, Mark Huhnen, Joginder Kaur, Elliott Greenhill, Jesmar Arevalo, Daisy Aigbe and Baudoin Mathix Mbiandji Ndipomi. Special thanks to Neelima Samaiya and Manuel Mouchipku.

Nathan Powell who facilitates any of the good creative work I do.

Rachel Taylor for not giving up on the play.

A shout-out to everyone at the Liverpool Everyman and a special thank-you to Mark Da Vanzo and Ashlie Nelson for being bold enough to programme this slightly bonkers play. It's massively appreciated and I hope it pays off.

Finally, a big thank you to Alf and Leo, for making me laugh every day.

J.W.M.

For my Mum and Dad

*And dedicated to the memory of
Curtis Warren Thwaites*

Characters

A
B
C

Any race or gender, the only important thing is that the cast is diverse.

This text went to press before the end of rehearsals and so may differ slightly from the play as performed.

Note on Play

This is a play about work.

That means there is a certain amount of work to do – for both the actors and the audience.

There are twenty-three scenes in this play but in each performance the audience will only see fifteen of them.

In each performance eight of the scenes that are performed are randomly selected by a machine or random-choice algorithm or app.

The actors only know which scene they will be playing when the machine has selected it.

The tabulated form of the play looks like this.

Scenes	A	B
1	**THE CAST**	
2	**THE LETTER**	
3	CHANGSHA. CHINA. 2015	DETROIT. USA. 2016
4	PARIS. FRANCE. 1844.	LONDON. ENGLAND. 1975.
5	**NOTTINGHAM. ENGLAND. 1816.**	
6	LIVERPOOL. ENGLAND. 1985.	HERTFORDSHIRE. ENGLAND. 2017.
7	MOSCOW. USSR. 1963.	LAGOS. NIGERIA. 2018.
8	**NOTTINGHAM. ENGLAND. 1816.**	
9	CHANGSHA. CHINA. 2015	DETROIT. USA. 2016.
10	GUAYAQUIL. ECUADOR. 1992.	HERTFORDSHIRE. ENGLAND. 2017.
11	**NOTTINGHAM. ENGLAND. 1816.**	
12	HERE. NOW.	HERE. THEN.
13	GUWAHATI. INDIA. 2023	SABRATHA. LIBYA. 2020.
14	**THE CAST**	
15	**NOTTINGHAM. ENGLAND. 1816.**	

The scenes in bold are non-negotiable, they are in every performance of the play.

The scenes that are subdivided into A and B columns will have one of those scenes in that row performed and then move on to the next numerical row. For instance, for the third scene the machine will either pick scene 3A or 3B. The next scene would then be either scene 4A or 4B – again randomly picked by the machine.

If you're simply reading the play you can arbitrarily decide which scenes you read as you progress through the play or flip a coin, etc.

However, if the play is being performed, the play requires that a machine or random choice generator (there are smartphone apps and websites for these) selects the scene. i.e. the autonomy lies with a machine or algorithm rather than a human.

Translations

Each of the scenes in which the characters would not be speaking English also contain a translated version of that scene. These translations can be projected as subtitles, or potentially the scenes could be played in those languages with subtitles being provided in English.

The Machine

The machine that selects the scene can be as simple or as complex as required.

It could be as simple as a smartphone with a random-choice-generator app that instantaneously selects and flashes up the scene to be played.

Or it could be a nightmarish, mechanised, loom-like device full of cogs and wheels that clanks and judders as it makes its choice.

Hopefully it is something that a designer and director can have fun with.

1. THE CAST

Lights up.

The actors are on stage. They use their real names.

There is room here to play and improvise around these lines and potentially mock the largeness of the idea, the natural waste in the scenes not witnessed by the audience and the amount of work that the play puts upon the actors. This is not obligatory, it's just an offer to find the humour and joy in this moment between cast and audience.

C	Hi
B	Hi
A	Hello.

Beat.

C	I'm Shaun
A	And I'm Menyee
B	And I'm Reuben.

Beat.

Tonight will be a story of stories

A	The stories of capitalism
B	And globalisation
C	And automation

Beat.

A	In this play there are over twenty different scenes
C	We each play dozens of different characters
B	In dozens of different stories
C	Different times

A	Different places
B	Different people
C	Some of the people you might know
B	Some of the people you definitely don't
A	Most of the stories that you see tonight
C	Will be selected randomly
B	By the machine

Pause.

A	So, we, the actors, won't know what scene we'll be playing until the machine makes its choice.
B	And the fact that it's random means there are actually two hundred and fifty-six versions of this play.

Pause.

That's a lot.

C	It's a fucking shedload
B	Some people could say, it's too much.
A	Not me.

Pause.

C	So, the play is pretty much guaranteed to be different every night.
B	Literally.
C	So this is a story of stories
A	Stories of capitalism
B	Globalisation
C	Automation
B	Money
C	Power
A	But mainly, it's the stories of work.
B	The stories of us.

2. THE LETTER

Complete darkness.

A voice. Potentially automated.

To the Gentlemen Hosiers of Nottingham and surrounding areas in the year of our Lord 1816.

Our lords and betters, we humbly appeal to you in this time of calamity and distress;

We are destitute of all the comforts of life – our only acquaintance being pinching poverty and pining want.

We wish to live peaceably and honestly by our labour;

And to train up our children in the paths of virtue and rectitude

But we cannot accomplish our wishes.

Thirty years ago, a silk-stocking maker obtained a decent subsistence.

No longer.

The twin evils of rising prices and new technologies means we have been overtaken and overridden, roughshod.

These new machines make our previous peaceable contentment impossible.

And we appeal to you, gentlemen, to put pressure on parliament regarding the death penalty for machine breaking.

Yes, machines have been broken. Looms have been tossed into the street.

But we are starving by inches, our children ever more so.

We wish to remind you that it is better to be content with a moderate profit than have your manufactories burnt to the ground.

Some of us have appealed to you through letter and some of our kin have recently been driven to take up arms and have met with the gallows' cold embrace.

There are men, women and children rising in every portion of the kingdom to replace them.

Those who have been lost will not die in vain.

Their cries will echo through this land.

So, let me make myself plain, there shall be no correspondence beyond this point.

If you comply with our previous requests, all will be well.

However, if not, I, Ned Ludd, and an army of men, women and children, who number in their thousands,

Will call upon you,

And if we cannot break looms we will break something else

And we will do it too, in spite of the Devil.

Yours,

A friend of the poor,

Ned Ludd

God Protect the Trade

3A. CHANGSHA. CHINA. 2015.

A and B are sat at computers. They are intently playing a computer game using keyboards. Possibly a large backdrop projection means we can see what they can see on the screen. B's avatar was trying to mine gold in the game but now is being attacked by a group of characters.

A 你今天做了什么?

What did you do today?

Pause.

你今天做了什么?

What did you do today?

B 滚开。

Fuck off.

A 在说我吗?

Me?

B 不是，我是说那些美国人。

No. I mean these Americans.

A 我知道。

I know.

B 他们是脑袋有问题对吧? 咱们彼此河水不犯井水。

I don't know what their problem is? I haven't done anything to them.

A 去冬泉谷走一趟吧，那里安静一点，昨晚我在那边找到黄金。

Take a trip to Winterspring, it's usually more quiet there, I mined gold there all last night.

B 没时间了，老板说要在四点前给他十万块黄金。

I haven't got time, boss said I have to get him a hundred thousand pieces of gold before four o'clock.

A 真搞不懂他们要这么多黄金来干嘛。

I really can't understand what they do with this gold.

B 他们把黄金卖给人。

They sell it.

A 这个我也知道，我是不明白那些买的人。他们要黄金来干嘛？

Yes I know that. What I can't understand is the person who buys it. What they do with it?

B 你可以在游戏中用黄金取得领先地位。很明显那些警卫根本不在乎这个，可是总有些懒得花时间玩游戏的美国胖子会想用这个方法。警卫把我们的黄金卖给他们换钱，然后那个美国人再用虚拟黄金买他们一直想要的虚拟宝剑。

The gold helps you to get ahead in the game. Obviously the guards don't care about getting ahead in the game but there's probably some fat American somewhere who can't be bothered to play the game for hours and hours. The guards sell our gold to them for real money and then the American uses that virtual gold to buy that shiny virtual sword they've always wanted.

A 他们良心过意得去吗？就这样坐享其成？

And they're happy with that are they? To get the reward without the work?

B 他们根本不介意。

Well. They're happier than us.

A 我才不会这么做。

一定不会。

Well. I won't do it.

I won't.

B 那你来动手吧。

Well, then maybe you should do it.

A 才不要，给人家惊喜才是我一贯的作风

No, I like to surprise people. That's my style.

B 那你要自己承担后果。

Then you have to bear the consequences yourself.

A 什么?

What?

B 你要承担后果。他今天在工厂里是这么说的,做不到就要承担后果。

You have to bear the consequences. He said it at the factory today, that anyone who can't do it will bear the consequences.

A 那是什么意思?

What's the meaning of that?

B 就是说 - 你要承担后果。

That is to say – you have to bear the consequences.

Pause.

A 他亲口告诉你的?

Is that how he told you?

B 也不算,虽然当时他在我旁边,但没有真的对着我说。说不定在跟我们其中一人说 吧,也有可能是跟全部人说,或者只是他在自言自语而已

No, he said it next to me right into the air, not really to me, maybe he's talking to one of us, maybe to all of us, or he's just talking to himself.

A 在吓唬吧。

Scary.

B 有被吓到吗?

Are you scared?

A 之前他们不让我假释,现在我天不怕、地不怕。

Since they told me I can't get parole I have decided to not be scared.

Pause.

你今天有到外面去吗?

Were you outside today?

B 没有,一整天都在工厂里。

No, all day in the factory.

A 那你一定有弄了些什么东西吧。

So, you made something.

B 对。

Yes.

A 在哪家工厂?

Which factory?

B 塑料厂。

Plastics.

A 要到外面去才能找到的哪一家吗?

Is that the one you have to go outside to get to?

B 也不用,走过楼道就到了

No, there's a corridor.

A –

They play on in silence.

你弄了些什么?

What did you make?

B –

A 你到底弄了些什么?

What did you make?

B 像只猫咪。

It was like a cat.

A 猫咪?

Like a cat?

B 很难跟你解释。

It's hard to explain.

A 试试看。

Try me.

B	我很累了。
	I'm tired.
A	我也累惨了，只是想说说话。
	I'm tired too but I like to talk.
B	是扁身的塑料猫咪。
	It was a flat plastic cat.
A	塑料猫咪?给这里做的?
	A flat plastic cat? For here?
B	不是，会送到别的地方去。
	No, to somewhere else.
A	我不明白。
	I don't understand.
B	–
A	你都在弄一些奇怪的东西，对吧?
	You make some weird things huh?
B	–
A	他们想要奇怪的东西。
	They want some strange things.
B	可能吧。
	I guess.
A	真猫尺寸?
	Real size?
B	什么?
	What?
A	跟真猫一样大，但扁的?
	The size of a real cat, but flat?
B	没有，就很小一只。
	No small, tiny.

A   细小扁身的塑料猫咪。

Tiny flat plastic cat.

B   –

A   是玩具吗?

A toy?

Beat.

B   笨蛋才会玩。

If the children are idiots.

A *laughs*.

就跟你说嘛,一点也不酷,很难跟你解释。

Told you. It's not cool and it's hard to explain.

A   你做了多少个?

How many did you make?

B   不要再聊了。

No more talking.

A   为什么?

Why?

B   别让我分心。

I need to focus.

A *snorts*.

A   专心这个? 闭着眼也没问题吧!

On this? You could do it with your eyes closed.

B   他们刚把我杀了,现在追不上进度,真的累死我了。

They killed me. I'm behind. And I'm tired.

Silence.

A   有没有试过意识到自己在做梦?

You ever have a dream and you know that you're dreaming?

B 什么?

   What?

A 我说你有没有试过在做梦时知道自己身处於梦境里?

   Do you ever have a dream and you know that you're dreaming?

   Beat.

B 有试过一次。

   Yes. I did. Once.

A 是怎样的梦?

   What was it?

B 我梦见自己飞起来了。

   I was flying in the air.

A 然后你突然醒觉自己根本不会飞。

   Then you suddenly realise that you can't fly.

B 对。

   Yeah.

A 那之后呢?就这样醒来了?

   What happened after that? Just woke up?

B –

A 梦醒了。

   You wake up.

B 也没有立刻醒来。

   Not straight away no.

A 发生什么事?

   What happened?

   Beat.

B   我从天上掉下来，一直在尖叫，感觉掉了很久。

I fell from the sky, screaming, for what felt like a thousand years.

A   –

B   大概就是那个感觉。

Well it felt like that.

Pause.

A   要是意识到自己在梦里，说不定可以改变情节，或者编写自己想要的梦境？

Do you think that if you can know that you're dreaming in a dream that you can, change a dream or, have a dream, that you want?

B   什么？

What?

A   你觉得我们可不可以创造自己想要的梦境？

Do you think we can make ourselves have the dreams that we want?

B   引导自己的思维。

Program yourself.

A   嗯嗯。

Mm-hmm.

B   不可以。

No.

Pause.

A   我一直想梦见下雪，但总是没办法。

I've been trying to dream of snow, but I can't.

B   这我也无能为力。

I don't know how I can help you.

THREE-A

A   这里太热了，要是能下雪那有多好。就算不能亲眼目睹，做梦看见心里也开。

It's so hot in here all I want is snow and I'll never see it and I would like to dream it.

B   –

A   我之前很讨厌下雪，但现在心裡总是惦著那些日子。

我想试吃一下

尝尝雪的味道。

I used to hate the snow. But now it's all I can think about.

All I can think about is eating it.

Tasting the snow.

B   你这蠢货，那有多脏你知道吗？

You defective product, the snow is dirty.

A   刚下的雪也脏吗？

Even from the sky?

B   特别脏。

Especially from the sky.

Silence.

A   这里实在是太热了。

It's too hot in here.

B   –

A   除了热就是闷，一点新鲜空气都没有，全是我们呼出来的废气不断在循环着。你有没有想过，这里的空气其实跟我们一样，快被这种苦闷给憋疯了。

And it's not just the heat it's the air. There's no air, all there is is the breath that's come out of you, and the breath that's come out of me, just cycling round. Cycling round and around and around. You ever think the air in here is as crazy and as bored as we are.

Pause.

B 没有想过。

No.

A 我有。

I do.

我相信万物都有灵。你听! 墙壁都在尖叫了。

I believe that everything has a spirit. And I think the walls are screaming.

B just looks at A.

B 或许你是时候要到外面走走了。

You could probably do with getting out of here for a bit.

A –

B 表现好一点，说不定会让你到工厂去。

Behave better and maybe you will be allowed at the factory.

A 才不要，我喜欢这里。

No, I like it here.

B 好吧。

Alright.

A 要维持原状。

It stays the same.

B 好吧。

Alright.

A 我只想白天有人在这里陪我。

I would just like someone to be here with me during the day.

Beat.

B 小陈

Chen

A 他怎么了？

What about him?

B 他很快就可以来这里陪你。

He'll be here with you during the day. Soon enough.

A 为什么？

Why?

B –

A 他又闯祸了？

He got in trouble again?

B 还没有。

Not yet.

A 他在说三道四？

Being a big mouth?

B 也不是。

No.

A 快告诉我。

Tell me.

Pause.

B *drops voice slightly.*

B 我在工厂看见过他。

I saw him in the factory.

A 你说过了，他坐在你对面。

Yes, he sits opposite, you told me.

B 他有一支笔。

He had a pen.

A 什么？

What?

B 他手里拿着一支笔。

He was holding a pen in his hand.

A 所以呢? 他是写诗的。

So? He's a poet. Was a poet.

B 他不该有笔的。

He should not have a pen.

A 工厂里都不能用笔的?

Were you not using pens in the factory?

B 不可以。

No.

A 噢。

Oh.

Beat.

他用笔来做什么? 写诗吗?

What was he doing with his pen? Writing a poem?

B *just looks at* A.

B 不是。

No.

Silence as they tap their keyboards.

The machine selects either Scene 4A or 4B.

3B. DETROIT. USA. 2016.

C You worried?

A Naw. You?

C Hell yes. You're sitting there trying to tell me you ain't scared?

A I mean, when the day comes, and obviously it's coming soon, I'll just have to learn how to do something else.

C Simple as that huh?

A Well, simple or not, it's gonna have to be done so…

C I'm too old to be that… calm about it.

A Mmm.

C I can't believe, I can't believe they do a thing like this.

A –

C You think of all the time and the effort and the work, and the money we made them, we…

Pause.

You went the meeting right?

A Yeah, I went the meeting.

C What's the new offer on the table again?

A The offer? Eleven dollars an hour.

C That for everybody?

A No, just for factory support but –

C But they've all been dropped.

A Yeah, all the wages been dropped yeah.

Beat.

C Eleven dollars an hour. I mean…

Beat.

What's the union say?

A   They saying they tried. They tried the best they could.

C exhales.

C   That's it? They tried?

A   Well what else do you want them to say?

C   Man, I remember when the unions used to, like, actually mean something. Now all they do is come back and say, they tried…

A shrugs.

They Chinese?

A   What?

C   The company, buying us out, they Chinese?

A   No. They're American. I mean they got people, departments all over the world but it's an American company, I mean it started here, it was founded here.

C   I don't get it.

A   What don't you get?

C   If they're American, how can they not, why don't they understand that

A   That it's not enough to live on.

C   Yeah.

Silence.

A   You mind if I show you something?

C   Go for it.

Grabs a heavy holdall and opens it up.

A   So my sister came up –

C   How is she?

A   Yeah, she's great, she just got a promotion, so you know, she's happy

C   Well that's great.

A	Well, yeah, I'm glad someone's happy, anyway. She came up, she helped me with this yard sale we had because of all this.
C	Okay.
A	And there were pieces that didn't get sold, I thought I'd bring them in and see if anyone wanted them.
C	Okay sure.
A	So, what have we got, we got, uh, okay there's this?
	C *pulls out a wrench*.
	You want this?
C	It's a wrench.
A	I know. You want it?
C	Let me see it.
	A *inspects it*.
	You been using this?
A	No. It's nearly new.
C	Nearly new. What the fuck is that?
A	–
C	Something is either used or new, so this is used.
A	Okay, it's been used, but not… so much.
C	I got a wrench but… okay.
A	Okay, great, so five dollars?
C	Five dollars?
A	Yeah.
C	You want five dollars from me for a used wrench when I've got a perfectly good used wrench sitting at home?
A	Name your price.
C	I didn't know you were tryna sell it me, I thought you were just trying to get rid of shit.
A	No, I wanna make some money.

C	Well, look who you're talking to.
	Pause.
A	Okay forget the wrench.
C	Okay.
A	Maybe, you would like, this.
	Pulls a stuffed toy from the bag. It's Barney the purple dinosaur from Barney & Friends.
	Pause.
C	The fuck is that?
A	It's Barney.
C	Okay. Let me rephrase, I know who the fuck it is what I wanna know is why you tryna give it to me?
A	Well it used to be Louisa's and I thought, maybe you could it give to your granddaughter?
	A *tosses it to* C.
C	A second-hand weak-ass purple dinosaur.
A	Well there's no need to get, personal.
C	No. There is. This is… this is… significant.
A	Is it?
C	I remember this guy. I remember Joshua watching this. I mean look at it. Look at it. What is this?
	Beat.
	What is it?
A	Barney?
C	No it's a Tyrannosaurus Rex. Fucking king of the dinosaurs and look what we've done to it.
A	–
C	Made it nice for kids and taken away its teeth. Taken away its power.
A	–

C	You don't find that fucking… relevant?
	Pause.
A	No.
C	No?
A	No, I just think, it's, you know, a toy.
C	Okay. Forget it. Let me try and be clear without being rude. I don't need your stuff, whether it's used or new or nearly fucking new or Barney, I don't need it. What I need is money. Or a new job. What I don't need is to give you my money for shit I don't need so that you then have my money.
A	Okay.
C	So you can put all this shit away.
	C tosses the purple dinosaur back.
A	Okay.
C	Put it away then.
A	–
C	–
A	Let me leave it out awhile, okay?
C	–
A	Let me feel like I'm trying, like I'm doing something.
C	–
A	Can't blame a guy for trying, is that not what they say?
C	Yeah. But also, you can't blame the other guy for saying no.
A	Okay.
C	Okay.
	Pause.
	I'm sorry man I'm just a bit stressed alright?

A   Of course. I get it.

Beat.

C   You think you could do me a favour?

Pause.

A   I ain't making no promises, you better tell me what it is.

They both laugh.

C   Okay. If, it snows tomorrow –

A   Snow?

C   Yeah, they said on the news that it might.

A   Okay.

C   Can you come pick me up?

A   Man, that ain't exactly on my route.

C   Please.

A   –

C   Please man.

　　I should have fixed my car last year, I know.

　　When things were a little bit better but you know I erm…

　　If it gets too cold it won't start, I know it, and erm…

A   Okay okay, I'll pick you up don't worry. 'Sfine.

Beat.

C   Thank you.

　　Coz if it does snow, that's me, that's me done. Seriously.

A   Okay.

　　It's okay.

Silence.

The machine whirrs into life.

The machine selects either Scene 4A or 4B.

4A. PARIS. FRANCE. 1844.

A and C are sat at a table. B is a waiter bringing out bread, olives, water, alcohol through the course of the scene.

A Die Kriminalitäts-, Raub- und Mordrate steigt steil. Und du weißt was das bedeutet, oder?

There is a rapid increase in crime, robberies, murder. And you know what this indicates don't you?

C Ja, natürlich, die –

Yes of course the –

A Die alte Ordnung fällt. Genau. So. Die Bourgeoisie wird verprügelt, mit Messern erstochen, beraubt – es ist das Gleiche, in der Tat noch schlimmer, in England. Und die Arbeiter überall auf der Welt verstehen nicht, dass was sie tun nichts anderes als eine Form von Protest ist. Und was ihnen gezeigt werden muss, ist dass wenn sie weiterhin nur als Individuen protestieren, ihre Mühen und Energie verschwendet sind. Aber wenn sie sich zusammen tun und zusammen als Menschen protestieren, dann wäre das…

The old order is falling away. Precisely. So. The bourgeoisie get beaten up, stabbed with knives, robbed – it is the same, in fact worse, in England. And the workers, the world over, do not realise that what they are doing is a form of *protest*. And what they need to be shown, is that if they continue to protest as *individuals* all their efforts and energy will be wasted but if they combined and protested together as *human beings* then that would be…

C Dann wäre das –

That would be –

A Kommunismus. Der Anfang davon.

Communism. The beginnings of.

C Auf jeden Fall.

Of course.

A and C beam at each other.

A   Ah. Ich kann dir gar nicht sagen wie gut das ist.

    Ah. I can not tell you how good this is.

C   Was ist?

    What is?

A   Dich hier zu haben. Direkt vor mir. In Paris. C'est magnifique.

    To have you here. In front of me. In Paris. C'est magnifique.

C   –

A   Ich fühle dass es jetzt passiert.

    I feel it will happen now.

C   Was passiert?

    What will?

A   Alles. Alles worüber wir gesprochen haben. Alles was wir geschrieben haben. Es passiert, so wie wir es geschrieben haben. Das ist das Gefühl das ich von dir kriege. Die Freude. Auf dem richtigen Weg zu sein und das zu wissen. Das ist das Gefühl das ich jetzt habe. Spürst du es auch?

    Everything. Everything we've talked about, everything we've written, it will all happen as we've written it. That's the energy I have from you. Just joy. To be on the right track and to know that you are on the right track. That is the energy I have just now. Can you feel it?

C   Ja.

    Yes.

A raises glass. C does same.

A   À votre santé.

C   À votre santé.

A   Oder wie sie in den Pubs in Manchester sagen: Cheers!

Or, as they say in the pubs of Manchester: Cheers!

C   Cheers.

A   Gar nicht mal schlecht. Musst noch am Akzent feilen.

Not bad. Accent needs work.

C   –

Pause.

A   Ah, das ist ein Leben, oder?

Ah. This is the life? No?

C   Solange ich in eine Bücherei kann, bin ich überall glücklich.

As long as I can get to a library I am happy anywhere.

A   Ah, Ich wünschte, ich könnte bleiben.

Ah, I wish I could stay.

C   Wie lange bleibst du?

How long are you here?

A   Zehn Tage, höchstens.

Ten days – at a push.

C   Und dann?

And then?

A   Köln, dann Barmen.

Cologne then Barmen.

C   Ah, der Familiensitz.

Ah the family seat.

A   Bitte.

Please.

C smiles.

Das hier ist tausendmal besser als die Fabrik in Manchester, aber die Fabrik in Manchester ist eine Millionen mal besser als zuhause in Barmen festzustecken.

This is a thousand times better than the factory in Manchester but then the factory in Manchester is a million times better than being stuck home in Barmen.

C   Ich erinnere mich, dass du das schon mal gesagt hast.

    I remember you saying.

A   Ja, aber ich glaube nicht, ich kann dir zur Genüge die Unterdrückung in all dem vermitteln. Wenn ich ausgehe, wird es missbilligt, weil ich offensichtlich Kommunisten treffe. Wenn ich in meinem Zimmer bleibe, wird lautstark missbilligt, dass ich offensichtlich Kommunistische Literatur schreibe. Ehrlich, ich kann nicht essen, trinken oder auch nur furzen, ohne ihre frommen Blicke auf mir zu spüren.

    Yes but I do not think I can convey to you strongly enough the oppressiveness of it all. If I go out they tut as I leave because obviously I'm meeting communists. If I stay in my room they tut loudly outside my door because I'm obviously writing communist literature. Honestly, I cannot eat, drink or let out a single solitary fart without having their pious eyes upon my face.

C   Na, du hast deine Freiheit hier und jetzt.

    Well you have your liberty here and now.

A   Nein! Hier im Hotel war ein Brief von meinem Vater.

    No! Here, at the hotel lay a letter from my father.

C   –

A   Und das ist das Ärgerliche. Er hört nicht zu. Mich hassen, meine politischen Ansichten hassen, von mir aus! Aber er hört nicht zu. Er weiß nicht mal was meine politischen Ansichten sind. Er verwechselt Kommunismus mit Liberalismus und schimpft dann über das Britische Parlament. Ich krieg sie drüber für die liberale britische Bourgeoisie. Es ist verrückt.

And this is the infuriating thing. He doesn't listen. Hate me, hate my politics, fine! But he doesn't listen! He doesn't know what my politics are! He confuses communism and liberalism and so in the letter scolds me about the goings-on of the British parliament! So there I am getting an earful on behalf of the bourgeois British liberals. It's insane.

C   Sagst du ihm das?

Do you tell him this?

A   Nein, ich beiß' mir auf die Zunge. So sehr es auch demütigend ist, Kommunist und Fabrikbesitzer zu sein, einem geschenkten Gaul schaut man nicht ins Maul.

No. I bite my tongue. As mortifying as it is to be both a communist and a factory owner I'm not stupid enough to look a gift horse in the mouth.

C   Selbstverständlich.

Of course.

C starts writing.

A   Was machst du?

What are you doing?

C   Eine Notiz schreiben.

Writing a note.

A   Wem?

To who?

C   Mich selbst.

Myself.

A   Aha! Inspiration!

Aha! Inspiration!

C   Nicht wirklich.

Not really.

A   –

C Hier steht lediglich: ‚Engels' Alter ist ein Schwein und wir müssen ihm einen schweineunhöflichen Brief schreiben.'

It simply reads. 'Engels' old man is a swine. And we must write him a swinishly rude letter.'

A *smiles*.

C ‚Lieber Friedrich Engels Senior, Sie unverbesserlicher, alter Schwachkopf…'

Mehr hab ich noch nicht.

'Dear Friedrich Engels Senior, you incorrigible old dunce…'

That's all I've got.

A Ein schöner Anfang. Danke.

It's a beautiful start. Thank you.

C Gerne.

You're very welcome.

A Also, ich habe eine Woche, vielleicht mehr. Lass uns trinken…

Right. Come on. I've got a week maybe more. Let's go get drunk.

C *nods*.

A (*Calling for* B.) L'addition s'il vous plaît!

Ich zahl' die Rechnung und du das Trinkgeld?

I'll get the bill if you pick up the tip?

C –

A Was?

What?

C –

A Nicht mal ein paar Centimen?

Not even a few centimes Karl?

FOUR-A

C   Im Moment bin ich etwas – in finanziellen Verlegenheiten.

   At the moment, I am somewhat, financially embarrassed.

A   –

C   Ich wollte dich ehrlicherweise noch in dieser delikaten Angelegenheit fragen, ob ich…

   In fact, I was going to ask you, at a somewhat more delicate juncture if truth be told whether I could…

A   Komm, erlaub' mir wenigstens noch, mich volllaufen zu lassen bevor du mich ausnimmst, ja?

   Come come, at least let me get pissed before you turn me upside down yes?

C   –

A   Und wenn ich derjenige bin, der zahlen muss, dann führ mich nur zu den billigsten Orten.

   And if I'm the one to be paying be sure to take me only the cheapest places.

C   Ich kenn' ja nur die billigsten Orte.

   I only know the cheapest places.

A   Touché. (*For* B.) L'addition s'il vous plait?!

   Beat.

   Und, warst du heute in der Bücherei?

   So did you visit the library today?

C   Ja.

   Yes.

A   Und hast du geschrieben?

   And did you write?

C   Selbstverständlich.

   Of course.

A   Lass mal hören.

    Can I hear it?

C   Ich hab's nicht dabei.

    I don't have it on my person.

A   Aber du erinnerst dich an das wesentliche?

    But you remember the gist?

C   –

A   Komm schon, was krieg ich denn für min Geld?

    Come on! Show me what my money gets me!

    Beat.

C   Also, ich hab' so im groben über das hier… nachgedacht…

    So, this is what I've been, roughly… musing.

A   Tu doch nicht so bescheiden Karl. Darin bist du nicht besonders gut.

    Stop feigning modesty Karl you're not very good at it.

C   Also.

    Sobald es Arbeitsteilung gibt, hat jeder Mensch nur einen bestimmten Tätigkeitsbereich, der ihm aufgezwungen wird und dem er nicht entkommen kann. Er ist ein Jäger oder Fischer oder Hirte oder Kritiker. Und das muss er bleiben, wenn er nicht seinen Lebensunterhalt verlieren will, also seine gesamte Existenz. In einer kommunistischen Gesellschaft aber, hat niemand einen eingeschränkten Tätigkeitsbereich. Jeder kann sich verbessern, in welcher Tätigkeit er wünscht. Die Gesellschaft reguliert die Produktion und macht es so möglich, dass ich heute dies tue und morgen jenes. Morgens jagen, nachmittags angeln, abends Rinderzucht und kritisieren nach dem Abendbrot. Gerade so wie ich es möchte, ohne je nur Jäger, Fischer, Hirte oder Kritiker zu werden.

Wie findest du das?

So.

So. As soon as the distribution of labour comes into being, each man has a particular, exclusive sphere of activity – that is forced upon him and he cannot escape it. He is a hunter, or a fisherman, or a herdsman, or a critic, and must remain so if he does not wish to lose his livelihood, that is, his very existence. However, in a communist society, nobody has one exclusive sphere of activity but each can become accomplished in any branch they wish. Society regulates general production and thus makes it possible for me to do one thing today and another thing tomorrow. To hunt in the morning, and to fish in the afternoon, rear cattle in the evening and criticise after dinner. Just as I wish, without ever *becoming* hunter, fisherman, herdsman or critic.

What do you think?

A   –

C   –

A   Ich liebe es. Wir werden nicht unser Beruf. Unser Wert ist nicht dadurch bestimmt.

       I love it. We do not become our occupation. Our worth is not defined by it.

C   Ganz genau.

       Precisely.

A   Wir bleiben frei.

       We remain free.

C   Ja, wir bleiben menschlich.

       Yes. We remain human.

A   –

C   –

       A *raises a glass. So does* C.

A   Auf's menschlich bleiben.
        To remaining human.
C   Auf's menschlich bleiben.
        To remaining human.
        B *comes out and puts the bill down.*
B   L'additon messieurs.
A   Merci.
C   –

        Beat.

        The next scene is Scene 5.

4B. LONDON. ENGLAND. 1975.

C is stood, and occasionally glances at notes.

A *and* B *are sat watching.*

C   What you find is, that if you look across the continent in France, you will find that they've been able to pay their managers less but get a much higher net taxed income. And the result has been that if, in fact, British companies put some of their top managers into Europe or elsewhere on French salaries at French levels of tax, they couldn't get them back because we couldn't in fact pay them a big enough gross salary to give them the net income.

   B*'s hand goes up.* C *ignores it and continues.* B*'s hand stays up.*

   Now, all of these in fact have been the economic effects of pursuing far too much equality, and I think we have very much now come to the end of the road. And, in fact, we find that the persistent expansion of the role of the state, beyond the capacity of the economy to support it, and the relentless pursuit of equality has caused, and is causing, damage to our economy in a variety of ways. It's not the sole cause of what some have termed the 'British sickness' but it is a major one.

   C *stares at* B *with hand up. It still doesn't go down.*

C   Yes?

B   Sorry to… I was just thinking about… jokes?

   Pause.

C   Jokes?

B   Yes.

C   –

B   Humour.

C   –

B Levity…?

Silence.

C I'm sorry William, who is this man?

Beat.

B Mrs Thatcher, I thought you knew I was attending, I'm James I –

C I'm not so much interested in who you are as why you are.

Beat.

A I asked him to pop by and listen to us –

C Why?

A Well, just before we leave for the States, I just wanted to make sure that we have the right, flavour.

C Flavour…

B I'm sure you know the line already ma'am, two countries separated by common language et cetera.

C To see if I'm legible?

A I wouldn't say… legible…

C Well, what would you say?

A Well, I would say, it's simply a matter of making sure we're understood across the –

C I've never been misunderstood in my life.

Beat.

A Well, I thought that perhaps it wouldn't hurt.

B (*Quietly.*) You may have overestimated that.

Pause.

C Where are you from?

B Michigan.

C Detroit?

B	No, ma'am I'm not that fortunate.
C	So you're from…
B	Lake Erie.
C	So you're from the backwaters of Michigan and you've been drafted in as a representative of the entire States of America to give notes upon my speech to the Institute of SocioEconomic Studies? Is that correct?
A	I wasn't given a lot of notice to be fair.
B	Thank you.
C	Do you know the Insitutue of SocioEconomic Studies? What it is? What it does?
B	No, but it sounds fancy.

Beat.

C	Let me tell you, James, I thank you for your concern but there is an excellent joke at the start and the rest simply takes care of itself.
B	Okay, I was merely thinking about, sweetening the pill.
A	A spoonful of sugar.
B	Precisely.
C	There will be no need for jokes. The medicine is sweet enough. Thank you.
B	Okay.

C makes to restart speech.

Can I hear it?

C	–
B	The joke? At the start. Is that okay?
C	–
B	That's why Bill asked me over right? As the authentic ear of America – or as close as you can get at late notice.

Pause.

C relents.

C   Only a week or two ago, Vermont Royster wrote that – and I quote – 'Britain today offers a textbook case on how to ruin a country.' I do take some consolation that there's only one small vowel sound between 'ruin' and 'run' a country. The small vowel sound is 'I'.

Pause.

A *laughs.*

B   Haven't you heard that already?

A   Yes but it's excellent every time.

B   Didn't you write it?

A   –

Pause.

B   It's very funny Mrs Thatcher. I'll listen to the rest of your speech now and stop clamouring for more jokes.

C *looks down at notes.*

C   Now, what are the lessons then that we've learned from the last thirty years? First, that the pursuit of equality itself is a mirage. What's more desirable and more practicable than the pursuit of equality is the pursuit of equality of opportunity. And opportunity means nothing unless it includes the right to be unequal and the freedom to be different. One of the reasons that we value individuals is not because they're all the same, but because they're all different. I believe you have a saying in the Middle West: 'Don't cut down the tall poppies. Let them rather' –

B*'s hand goes up.*

Pause.

Yes.

B   I think it would be more common to say Midwest.

C   I'm not very common.

B   Well usual then.

Beat.

C	That too.
	Pause.
A	Is that what the Yanks would say then is it? Midwest?
B	Generally, yeah.
A	Might be worth considering then?
C	No. Middle. I shall say middle.
A	–
B	Am I still getting paid for this?
A	Later.
C	Do you mind terribly if we could get to the end of this? If we could finish it, finish the actual thing?

C scans notes.

…First, that the pursuit of equality itself is a mirage. What's more desirable and more practicable than the pursuit of equality is the pursuit of equality of opportunity. And opportunity means nothing unless it includes the right to be unequal and the freedom to be different. One of the reasons that we value individuals is not because they're all the same, but because they're all different. I believe you have a saying in the Middle West: 'Don't cut down the tall poppies. Let them rather grow tall.' I would say, let our children grow tall and some taller than others if they have the ability in them to do so. Because we must build a society in which each citizen can develop his full potential, both for his own benefit and for the community as a whole, a society in which originality, skill, energy and thrift are rewarded, in which we encourage rather than restrict the variety and richness of human nature.

Looks up. C is finished.

Pause.

That's a broad smile William. Why?

A	You're brilliant. They'll love you.

Pause.

B   Yeah. They will.

Pause.

The next scene is Scene 5.

5. NOTTINGHAM. ENGLAND. 1816.

C   Gracing us with your presence?

B   Eh?

C   You coming?

B   –

C   The hunt John.

Pause.

B   Is that what they're christened it?

C   They have.

B   –

C   –

B   What?

C   Are you coming John?

Pause.

John.

B   No.

Beat.

C   They won't receive that well John.

B   –

C   I can tell you that.

B   –

C   You cannot go the meetings and not go the hunt.

B   Why?

C   –

B   Why?

C   Has someone boxed your ears? Have you fallen off a fucking horse?

B	–
C	I could stand here naming reasons John but the main one is it's something a traitor would do. Or a coward.

Pause.

So. You're coming then. |
| B | No. |
| C | I'm not asking.

Pause.

These men are not for fucking about, John. |
B	They don't know who I am, we were all –
C	Everyone knows who everyone is. Especially you.
B	–
C	Fucking size of yer. And you fucking stoop. My boy says you look like the old oak in back of the Thomases' house you're that hunched.
B	Nice of him.
C	I'm just saying, they know you were there, they expect you to come, so, come…

Pause.

You're coming. |
B	–
C	They're not fucking about.
B	–
C	Why come the meetings if you're not gonna go on the fucking hunt!
B	I agree with them, I do agree with them. In the principle of it just not the, the action.
C	And what in flaming hellfire is principle without action?
B	–

C	It's nowt John. It's neither one thing or t'other. It's a wet fart.

Beat.

B	'Snicely phrased that.
C	I haven't got your words John.
	We know that.
	But sometimes words stop and action starts.
	So I haven't got words but I do have courage.
	And I know you do too.
	Especially now.

Silence.

John.

B	Yes. Yes.

Pause.

C	We won't get this chance again.
	Soldiers on their way up from London, here end of the week.
	They're recruiting boys in Mansfield now an' all. For the knowledge.
B	They won't get anything out of that.
C	People are starving John. Do fucking oat for a crust.
B	–
C	You can't imagine it no?
B	No.
C	And five year ago, if I'd a said that you'd be stood there, a big fucking bag of skin and bone, watching a machine take your work, would you have been able to imagine that?
B	–

C Take your work to do it half as well. And men, Englishmen, would pay for that whilst you sit there and starve. Would you have been able to imagine that, John?

Silence.

Speak to me then. What is ailing you?

B –

C No one's going to harm the Thomases.

B Well that's –

C Just their looms John. Just their fucking looms. That's it. You heard tell of what they're doing in France and we're just breaking a few fucking looms. There's plenty want to break more than that.

B –

C And think on it though. Think on it. Picking up a big fucking hammer and just smashing it straight through the very source of your pain.

B –

C Imagine that.

B –

C Can you not feel it John? Can you not hear it? I can fucking smell it me. Can fucking taste it. Think about it every night.

B –

C Chance won't be coming again.

B –

C There's looms going in everywhere. Bullwell, Yorkshire, Manchester.

Manufactories springing up by the day.

If we don't act, by the time our, the kids... they won't even know there was a choice, they won't even know there was a fight to be had.

It'll just occur to them as... fact, the natural order of things...

The trade won't exist and so we won't exist.

Need to do it now before soldiers come and the weather changes.

B   What's the weather do?

C   Were you not listening last night? Snow's coming. Can't do nowt then. Tracks lead straight back to your home.

So we have to do it now.

Tonight.

Before the soldiers, before the snow.

Pause.

The machine whirrs into life.

The machine selects either Scene 6A or 6B.

6A. LIVERPOOL. ENGLAND. 1985.

A   Everything okay?

C   Yeah.

A   Tell your face then lad.

C   It's boring.

A   What is?

C   Cleaning.

A   I know but if you don't get all the grime, cobwebs and shit up now then there's no way to sort it later. Your alpha is your omega here mate.

C   What?

A   If you want the job to end well, you need it to start properly.

C   Yeah.

A   You know what I do? I don't think of it as cleaning, I think of it as prep.

C   Why?

A   Coz no one likes fucking cleaning do they? But if you call it prep, makes it that bit easier.

C   Does it?

A   Yeah, don't think 'I'm cleaning the room' think 'I'm prepping the room'.

C   I'm prepping the room.

A   Yeah.

C   Alright. I'll give that a try, see what it does.

A   –

C   I've done it now anyway.

A   What?

C   I've, prepped, the room.

A Have yer?

C Yeah.

A Have you fuck.

C I've been in here for like three hours Mick.

A Unfortunately the length of time you've spent in a room is not synonymous with the amount of work you've done in a room is it?

C What?

A Look at that.

C Where?

A Up there.

C Well, it's a bit –

A Yeah, just a bit.

C Well no one's gonna notice that

A When you come into a room, a part of you knows whether it's spanking clean or a bit grotty without even having to look. You clock it regardless.

C So I need to do that top corner again?

A Again? Have you even done it once?

C –

A –

C –

A Jase, why have I given you this room?

C Coz it's the dirtiest, dustiest one and I'm an apprentice and you're a shithouse.

A Well yeah there's always that. Look at this.

C –

A I shifted this wardrobe out for you this morning, have you had a look round the back of it?

C	No, what is it?
	B *sticks their head in.*
B	Michael. Do you want a tea?
A	Oh yes please, that would be lovely thank you.
B	How do you take it?
A	Just a bit of milk and leave the bag in.
B	Leave the bag in?
A	Yes please.
B	Right. And Jimmy?
C	Jason.
B	Jason, sorry, would you like a tea?
C	No, thanks.
B	Right, I'll be back in a bit with yours Mike.
A	Thank you.
	B *leaves.*
	What are you doing?
C	What?
A	Is that the first time she's seen yer?
C	Pretty much, yeah.
A	And she's offered you a cup of tea?
C	Yeah?
A	And you've said no??
C	So?
A	If you say no the first time a tea is offered the likelihood is they're not gonna come back round and ask you again.
C	–
A	You're setting up the pattern of the relationship. You're doing yourself out of tea.

C	But I don't like tea. I only like cold drinks.
	A sighs and shakes head in resignation.
A	Just go on have a look behind this wardrobe then.
C	Who's round the back of it? Aslan?
A	Just have a look you divvy.
C	There's nothing there?
A	You see that there though.
C	Yeah.
A	So, whatever blert did the previous job, he couldn't be arsed to shift the wardrobe properly so he's just moved it out a bit and did the bare minimum right.
C	Well, it's not that different a colour, I'll just go over it. Not a massive problem is it?
A	Yeah but that's not why I'm showing you it.
C	–
A	Have a look at it. The bit they didn't do, the bit they left.
C	Yeah.
A	Have a feel of that.
C	–
A	Go on, have a feel of it, the finish of it.
C	–
A	See the difference, you feel the difference of that?
C	–
A	The difference between the job the blert's done and this?
C	–
A	Ey?
C	–

A   Have a feel.

C   –

A   Can you feel that?

C   –

A   That is lovely that. That is real, that's quality, no brush marks nothing like, it's like glass.

C   –

A   See, there's certain things that are commonly believed to be more difficult. Plastering, being a sparks, all of that, yeah.

Everyone accepts that painting, decorating is a piece of piss and that's why so few people are any good at it.

Any dickhead can get a brush and lash a bit of paint about.

But that's not the same as being a painter and decorator.

So when I saw the patch behind that wardrobe that's why I chucked you in here, so you could learn… well what is it I want you to learn… like, an appreciation I s'pose

Like an appreciation of the difference

Between just doing the job and having a craft.

C   –

A   Have a feel. Can you feel that now though?

C   Yeah. I think I can.

A   –

Pause.

The machine whirrs into life and selects either Scene 7A or 7B.

6B. HERTFORDSHIRE. ENGLAND. 2017.

C *and* B *are six-year-olds.*

Silence.

C   Do you want to play that the floor is lava?

B   No.

Silence.

C   Do you want to play computer?

B   What games have you got?

C   I've got Minecraft.

B   I don't really like Minecraft.

C   What about Warcraft?

B   My brother says that Warcraft is for complete geeks.

C   No it's not. My night elf hunter's costume is completely orange and it's really cool.

B   Orange?

C   Yeah!

B   Is that your favourite colour?

C   Yeah.

B   That's weird. A favourite colour is like blue or red or something. Not orange.

C   I think a favourite colour can be anything you want… I mean as long as it's a colour obviously.

Pause.

       What time do you get collected?

B   Don't know.

C   Is it your dad collecting you?

B   Yeah.

C   After work?

B	He doesn't go to work.
C	How can he not go to work?
B	He's not very well.
C	Is that why he looks like that?

Beat.

B	I think so yeah.

Pause.

C	So if he doesn't work then, what does he do all day then?

Beat.

B	He looks after me. And he sleeps a lot.
C	He had to sit down at the top of the stairs.
B	Yeah, I know.
C	And he shakes.
B	Yeah I know.
C	I think he'll get better.
B	I think that too but I don't say it to him.
C	And when he does, then he could get a job with my dad. He works on the rig, well not on the rig but he goes there, he helps with the massive drill they've got…
B	Yeah.
C	Really massive drill going into the sea. I bet it goes brrrrrrrrrrrrrrrrrrrrrrrrrrr.

C *vibrates, impersonating the drill.*

Brrrrrrrrrrrrrrrrrrrrrrrrrrrr.

B	–
C	You do it! Brrrrrrrrrrrrrrrrr.
B	Brrrrrrrrrrrrrrrrrrrrr.

C	Brrrrrrrrrrrrrrrrrrrrrrrr.

They are drills together. Enjoying it.

And then if your dad was on the rig you could have a garden like us.

Beat.

B	Yeah.

Pause.

C	I liked your balcony. Just you can't play football on it.
B	I play football on the balcony sometimes.
C	It's not the same. Here we have a tree for a post and for the other post my dad just puts down a golf flag.

A *enters.*

A	Are you two okay?
C	Yes.
B	Yeah.
A	No funny business?
C	No we're being very good Mummy.
A	Now Ashley what things do you like to eat?
B	I like pizza.
A	I've made goulash. Is that okay? Do you like goulash?

Beat.

B	Yes.
A	Great.
C	I love goulash.
A	You sound like you're being very quiet and very good, what are you up to?
C	We're talking about Daddy's job.
A	Of course you are. Food will be ready soon.

A leaves.

Beat.

C   Brrrrrrrrrrrrrrrrrrrrrrrrrrr.

B   –

C   And do you know what they dig up with the massive drill?

B   No.

C   Oil.

B   I think I did know that actually.

C   And do you what oil actually *is*?

B   What?

C   It's dead dinosaurs.

B   Dead dinosaurs?

C   Isn't that crazy?

B   Does someone kill them?

C   No. They've obviously been dead for years and then they just… turn into oil.

B   Yeah.

C   So oil is just like Raptors and Stegosauruses and like that one with the bony ball on its tail –

B   Ankylosaurus.

C   Yeah!

B   So cool.

C   So basically, if we didn't have dinosaurs we wouldn't have cars.

Pause.

I want to be someone who finds dinosaur bones when I'm older. With the tiny brushes.

B   Yeah. I wanna be a footballer. And then at night I wanna be in the circus.

C	Like a clown?
B	Yeah, like a clown. Or an acrobat.
C	An acrobat would be better for football.
B	Oh yeah.

Pause.

C	What shall we play then?
B	I'm not sure.

Beat.

C	I know what we should play.
B	What?
C	We should play… I think we should play… tag!

C *taps* B.

You're it.

B	No you're it!

B *taps* C *and runs away.*

C *chases* B *round and through the machine until* B *bumps into the machine or some kind of stand – a china plate, white with a blue design, placed high up, rolls and falls and smashes.*

C	Ohhhhhh.
B	Shit.
C	Whoa! That is a rude word.
B	–
C	I'm going to have to tell on you.
B	Why? Because I said…
C	No. Because you did that.
B	I didn't, mean to, we, we were playing.
C	Mummy is going to be so upset.

B —

C It cost a lot of money she said.

It costs a lot because it's old.

They stare forlornly at the smashed plate.

The machine whirrs into life. The machine selects either Scene 7A or 7B.

7A. MOSCOW. USSR. 1963.

A   Ты сделала работу?

Did you do the work?

C   Да

Yes.

A   И какое время удержания плазмы?

And what was the plasma confinement time?

C   Девять миллисекунд.

Nine milliseconds.

A   И конечная температура?

And the final temperature?

C   Сто пятьдесят миллионов градусов.

One hundred and fifty million degrees.

A   А ты всё это скопировала?

And you've copied it all down?

C   Да.

Yes.

A   В обеих книгах?

In both books?

C   Да.

Yes.

A   Отлично. Теперь мы можем поесть.

Fine. We can have lunch.

They get out containers for lunch.

C   Ты читала новости? Валентина Терешкова?

You read the news? Valentina Tereshkova?

A   Конечно.

Yes of course.

C   Какое замечательчое достижение, не правда ли?

　　 What a wonderful achievement no?

A   Да.

　　 Yes.

C   Ты не впечатлена?

　　 You're not impressed?

A   Впечатлена.

　　 I'm impressed.

C   А женщина?

　　 And a woman?

A   –

C   Ты когда-нибудь думала, что доживёшь до этого дня? Первая женщина в космосе и она – женщина Совета?

　　 Did you ever think you would live to see the day? The first woman in space and she is a Soviet?

A   Я даже никогда не думала об этом.

　　 I never even thought about it.

C   Я так горда. Женщина в космосе, то имеет большое значение, не прабда ли? О равенстве, которое мы имеем здесь?

　　 It makes me proud. A woman, it sends a real message doesn't it? To the world – about the equality we have.

A   Я не уверена, что женщина, у которой к заднице привязаны двести семьдесят четыре тонны ракетного топлива, и вырошенной в стратосферу является лушим показателем равенства.

　　 I'm not sure a woman having two hundred and seventy-four tonnes of rocket fuel strapped to her arse and being shot out of the stratosphere is the best indicator of equality.

C	–
A	Извините. Я – устала.
	I'm tired. I'm sorry.
	A unwraps some food. So does C.
C	Конечно устала. Ты много работаешь.
	Of course you're tired, you're working hard.
A	Мы все много работаем.
	We're all working hard.
	Beat.
C	Хочешь?
	Would you like this?
A	Что это?
	What is it?
C	Шарлотка.
	Sharlotka.
A	Нет. У тебя только одна.
	No you only have one.
C	Пожалуйста
	Have it.
A	Мы можем разрезать…?
	We can cut it…?
C	Нет. Похалуйста. Возьми.
	No just have it.
A	Уверана?
	You sure?
C	Да.
	Yes.
	Pause.

A   Спасибо. Ты очень добра.

Thank you. That is real kindness.

C   –

A takes it. Puts in front of themself.

A   Знаешь моё мнение?

You know what I think?

C   –

A   Это я думала, когда я читала новости.

I thought it this morning, when I read the news.

C   –

A   По-моему, проще Валентину Терешкову отправить в космос, чем заставить Николая поднять один носок.

I think, as difficult as it is, it is easier to send Valentina Tereshkova into space than it is for me to get Nikolay to pick up one sock.

Beat.

Один носок!

One sock!

Pause.

По-моему это лучшее сравнение.

And I think that might be the better measure.

C   –

A   Да. у нас женщина на орбите, но можем ли мы заставит моего мужа поднять один носок?

Yes we have a woman in orbit but can we get my husband to pick up a sock?

C   –

A   Сталин не мог управлять этим и поэтому, я думаю, что Хрущев тоже не сможет.

	Stalin could not manage it and so I don't think Khrushchev will be able to either.
C	Хрущев просто переставит вещи. Ты в конечном итоге будешь поднять штаны Николая вместо носков.
	Khrushchev will just rearrange things. You will end up picking up Nikolay's pants instead.
A	Это я уже делаю.
	I already do.
C	Неужели? И штаны тоже?
	Pants too! Oh no!
	A *and* C *laugh*.
A	Это то же самое для всех женщин этих мучин. Ленин, Сталин, Хрущев, держу пари, никто из них не поднимет штаны. Все Политбюро говорит о равенстве и свободе, но ни один из них не оборачивается и не поднимает штаны.
	I bet it is the same for all the women of these men. Lenin, Stalin, Khrushchev, I bet not one of them picks up their pants. The whole politburo talks of equality and freedom and yet not one of them turns around and picks up their pants.
	A *and* C *laugh*.
	B *enters*.
B	Что за шутка?
	What's the joke?
C	Нууу…
	Mmm…
B	Шутка?
	The joke?
C	Ничего.
	Oh nothing.

B Давай.

   Go on.

A Ну ладно. Итак, Американец, Француз и Россиянин остались одни на необитаемом острове. Они ловят рыбу для пропитания и внезапно ловят золотую рыбку, которая обещает исполнить два желания для каждого в обмен на ее свободу.

   Американец: "Я хочу миллион долларов и вернуться домой!"

   Француз: "Я хочу трёх красивых женщин и вернуться домой!"

   Россиянин: "Тщ! Но мы так хорошо ладили! Три ящика водки и двоих парней верни!"

   Okay. So. An American, a Frenchman and a Russian are alone on an uninhabited island.

   They catch fish for food and suddenly catch a Golden Fish, who promises to fulfil two wishes for each in return for her freedom:

   The American: 'A million dollars and to go back home!'

   The Frenchman: 'Three beautiful women and to go back home!'

   The Russian: 'Tsk, and we were getting along so well. Three crates of vodka and the two fellas back!'

   A and C laugh.

B Вы смеялись такой старой шутке?

   You were laughing at this old joke?

A Да.

   Yes.

C Да.

   Yes.

B Неужели?

Really?

A Надо смеяться где можешь.

You have to laugh where you can.

B Правда. Вы читали новости? Валентина Терешкова?

This is true. Did you read the news? Valentina Tereshkova?

C Читала. Отлично, не правда ли?

I know. Amazing isn't it?

B Да.

Yes.

A Никогда не думала, что доживу до этово дня. Слава Советской власти.

I did not think I would live to see the day. Glory to Soviet power.

B Слава Советской власти.

Glory to Soviet power.

C Слава Советской власти.

Glory to Soviet power.

Pause.

B Шарлотка?

Sharlotka?

A Да. Это не кажды день у нас есть женщина-космонавт.

Yes. Not every day that we have a female cosmonaut.

B –

A Хотите?

Would you like it?

B   Нет. Это для вас.

    No. You have it.

A   Нет.Пожалуйста. Это для вас.

    No, please, you.

B   Уверена?

    You are sure?

    A nods.

    Это для меня?

    Really?

A   Да. Абсолютно. Мне достаточно.

    Yes. Oh yes. I've had enough.

    Pause.

    The next scene is Scene 8.

7B. LAGOS. NIGERIA. 2018.

B   Did you do the work?

A   –

C   Of course she did the work.

A   –

C   She always does the work.

A   No, I don't.

C   –

B   Why are your grades always so high then?

A   Because I have a level of intelligence you can't… comprehend.

        C *laughs*.

        –

C   Tell her the thing you were saying to me before

A   –

C   Tell her.

A   So I was saying – what?

B   What?

A   You're smiling already

B   I cannot smile?

C   Go on!

A   But why is she smiling?

B   Because I know it's going to be smart, I can feel it.

A   So I was saying, you know there is, a historical delineation between AD and BC…

        C *starts laughing at* B.

        So basically AD is our modern era –

B   I know what AD and BC are!

A	Okay okay, I'm just checking.
B	If I hear BC I just think… a very very long time ago.

C *laughs*.

A	Okay that's fine –
C	Just say what you said –
A	So I was saying in the future, I think, there will be a demarcation, that will be called BI and AI.
B	AI as in –
A	No, not that, what it will be is After Internet – AI.
B	–
A	Because it will change how we look at history. There will be a before and an after.
B	I think people overstate how important the internet is.
A	Okay. So, what happened to the Erie tribe in 1659?
B	What?
A	What happened to the Erie tribe in 1659?
B	Where?
A	America.
C	It's always America.
B	She's just wants to tell us how cool Manhattan is again.
A	No. Seriously, what happened to the Erie tribe in 1659?
B	Of course I don't know.
A	And why don't you know?
B	Because I don't know. No one has told me. I / haven't read
A	And what if I said to you that no one could tell you what happened to the Erie tribe in 1659.
B	Then I would say that your question is… nonsensical.

A   Why?

B   Because, because I don't know, and if there is no one to tell me the answer then…

A   Then…

B   Then there is no answer. There is nothing to be known.

A   But there is something to be known. There was definitely a group of people who had, or maybe were given, that name. A missionary priest mentions them in 1656, that they are involved in a war revolving around the fur trade with Europeans. And then that's it. They are never mentioned again. So, what happened to them?

B   Well they, I don't know, they… died?

A   Yes, that group of people is classified as extinct.

Pause.

B   But what I think is…

A   Yes.

B   I don't know you know, if you can only tell me that they were there and then they were not…

C   And nothing else.

B   Yeah.

C   –

B   Then I don't know how to… it's like a riddle.

C   Mm.

B   Like is it even…

A   Important?

B   Yeah?

A   Well, how important is it when a group of people, a culture, dies?

Pause.

B   Well of course it is but if it can't even be known, what exactly happened. / Then

A   Is Independence Day important for you?

B   Of course.

A   Why?

B   Because it's our history. It's important.

A   And what if… it had happened but no one had told you about it.

B   It would still be important even if someone didn't know, even if I didn't know.

A   And what if no one knew about it, no one talked about it.

B   But it had still happened?

A   Yes.

B   –

A   Would it still be important?

B   Of course.

A   Why?

B   Because it had still…

C   Happened.

B   Yeah.

A   Exactly. But what happened to the Erie doesn't matter to you for exactly the same reasons. It happened but no one knows.

B   –

A   I'm not trying to make you feel bad.

B   Oh okay.

       C *laughs*.

A   I'm just saying that history is just the record of the records.

B   –

A	And if you have the records – or are in the records – you are in history. And if, if you don't, then you are not. And that's why there will be a historical equivalent of before internet and after internet because, because it will record everything.
C	Too smart.
B	I know.
C	How does this stuff even occur to you?
A	I was watching a documentary –
C	Oh so you were relaxing.

B *and* C *laugh*.

A It was documentary about Syria and all these different types of people trying to go to Europe the back way.

And there's a bit where, it's shot from above, in a helicopter, at night, infrared. This little boat sets off from the coast and after just a few moments it catches fire.

You see everyone jump off, some look like they have flames on them but then flames go out in the water.

I'd never seen it before and yet it looked familiar to me. And I was wondering why does it look familiar? And then I thought, it's on the internet, that's why.

How many videos of bodies on fire are there on the internet?

Pause.

Uncountable and yet they are being counted.

Unlike the Erie.

Where did they go?

Silence.

The next scene is Scene 8.

8. NOTTINGHAM. ENGLAND. 1816.

C   What did you make to that then ey?

B   –

C   What did you make it?

B   –

C   I tell you what it was.

       It was the grandest night of our lives.

       Did you not think?

       You know what I keep thinking about? What I keep hearing?

       The boots in the dark.

       All them boots just tramping in the dark.

       How many boys?

       How many villages?

       How many villages was that John?

       How many boots John?

       Just that noise.

       Silence and boots and flame.

       And the weight of it.

       The weight of us. All of us.

       The weight and the silence and the boots.

       And the pure weight of that hammer.

       What a thing that was.

       The weight of the hammer and the silence and then the swing.

       The swing of it.

       The sound of it.

       To take a hammer to that machine,

       That big beautiful bastard of a machine,

That big beautiful bastard machine

To hear it crunch and crack

And keen and weep

And cry out in the dark

And finally silence.

Holy

Golden silence

Every loom broken.

And imagine if every loom int' country were broken

Each and every one of them dead in the street,

Good for nowt except kindling.

Never to be rebuilt

Reborn

I looked down the street after

It was like I could feel the work flowing back to me

Coming down the street toward me

Easing off the hills

Running down into the Trent

And flowing toward me

Into the holes of me boots

The pride flowing in.

Pause.

And the rightness of it John,

The justice

To swiftly murder that which aims to kill you.

To say no more, that's it, done, farewell.

Fuck me it were good!

And now

And now it begins

It has begun

The echoes of this will ring out.

They'll be talking about it in Bulwell and Basford and Mansfield.

And then across Nottinghamshire.

Then Derby

It will spread east and south and west and north

And it will ring out and out and out.

Across England.

And they'll say that this was an important day.

The day we stood up

Were counted

The day the weavers stood and said weavers weave, work is what makes us

And we shan't be parted

Not just for us

But for our children John

And every fucker else.

C stops.

Silence.

What ails you then?

You not in agreement?

B   No. I am.

C   Aye. You should be.

Silence.

I saw you John.

B	–
C	We all saw you.
B	–
C	'Twasn't exactly subtle.
B	–
C	A man your size can't stay that still for that long.
B	–
C	I mean you're big but no one's going to mistake you for an actual fucking tree.
B	–
C	What happened?
B	–
C	Never seen you scared before.
B	–
C	Always mouthing off when we were little.
B	–
C	Fear then. The fear cut you. *Shakes head.* What was it then?
B	–
C	Because I had to defend you. They were like what the fuck were that. The others. So I said to the lads, John is not a coward, Our John is not a coward. I had to defend yer. It wasn't easy John.
B	–

C	What was it? Tell me.

	You can tell me.

	Pause.

B	I could hear the children. The Thomas children crying.

	Pause.

C	I know but nowt happened to them John. No one did oat to them.

B	–

C	John. No one did nothing to 'em.

	They was just scared.

	And rightly so.

	But they was just scared, not hurt, not starving.

B	I know. But I could hear 'em crying.

	Silence.

	C *hugs* B.

C	I know brother. I know. You did right. You did right. It's all fine. You did your bit.

	C *looks at* B.

	The machine whirrs and selects either Scene 9A or 9B.

9A. CHANGSHA. CHINA. 2015.

B and A are at their computers. We can potentially see a projection of the game they are playing where they are mining gold.

They play in silence for a while.

B   我想要一件这样的披风。

            I want a cloak like that.

A   披风?

            Cloak?

B   那件橘色的披风。

            The orange cloak.

A   在游戏里用?

            In the game?

B   那当然!

            Of course!

A   还以为你想在这里穿。

            I thought you were saying for here.

B   在牢房里穿橘色披风来干嘛?

            What would I do with an orange cloak in prison?

A   你也有道理。

            Fair point.

            Beat.

            你是说影月毁灭者披风?

            You mean the Shadowmoon Destroyer Cloak?

B   对,就是它了。

            Yes. That's the one.

A   你真会挑!

            You sure know how to pick!

B　　谢谢。

　　　Thank you.

A　　捡起它能大大提升攻击力和致命重击。

　　　It binds when it's picked up and it really increases your attack power and critical strike.

B　　而且它很好看。

　　　But also, it's pretty.

A　　–

B　　穿起来一定很漂亮。

　　　And if I wore it I would feel pretty.

　　　Beat.

A　　你是说很帅气是吧?

　　　Do you not mean handsome?

B　　不是，漂亮跟帅气是两回事。那怕只是几秒钟，我也想漂亮一下。

　　　No pretty. Pretty and handsome are different things. And just for a few moments, a few seconds, I would like to feel pretty.

　　　They play on in silence.

A　　你今天在哪家工厂?

　　　What factory were you in today?

B　　纺织厂。

　　　Textiles.

A　　那你确实有到外面去!

　　　Ah, so you went outside!

B　　有啊。

　　　Yes.

A　　今天天气如何?

　　　What was the weather like?

NINE-A 85

B　　阳光普照。

Sunny.

Beat.

A　　你弄了些什么？

What did you make?

B　　–

A　　你今天弄了些什么？

What did you make today?

B　　我真的很累了，现在只想多找一点黄金，然后去休息一下。

I'm tired. I just want to focus on getting the gold and then lying down.

A　　我也累惨了，只是想说说话。

I'm tired too but I like to talk.

B　　–

A　　你不打算告诉我吗？

You're not going to tell me?

B　　对。

No.

Pause.

A　　不然这样好了。如果我能猜中你昨天的工作，你要说你今天到底弄了什么？

好不好？

How about this?

How about if I guess what you made yesterday then you have to tell me what you made today?

How about that?

A produces a red tissue-paper crown, the kind that you find in a UK Christmas cracker and puts it on top of their head. A *sits smiling and proud; waiting for the inevitable laugh when* B *looks.* B *doesn't look.*

我想我知道了。

I bet I can guess.

B　—

A　小傅。

Fu.

B　—

A　我知道你昨天到底弄了什么!

I bet I can guess what you made yesterday!

B　—

A　小傅。

Fu.

B　—

A　小傅。

Fu.

B　—

A　小傅。

Fu.

B　—

A　小傅!

Fuuuuuuuuuuuu!

B　搞什么鬼?

What the hell?

B *finally looks at* A.

从哪里找来的?

Where did you get that?

A　　你可不是我唯一的朋友。
You're not my only friend.

B　　我他妈的是!赶快把它拿掉!
I fucking am. Get that off your head now.

A　　我不要。
No. I don't want to.

B　　要是被狱卒看到，他们会打死你的。
If the guards see it, they'll destroy you.

A　　我不管，我才不怕。
I don't care. I'm not scared.

B　　立刻拿掉!
Off. Now.

A　　那告诉我你今天弄了些什么?
Tell me what you made today then.

B　　把东西拿掉，我就告诉你!
Okay. Take it off and I will!

A　　好吧。
Okay.

A daintily takes the paper hat off.

好了，小傅，你今天到底弄了什么?
So, Fu, what did you make today?

B shakes their head.

B　　今天弄了毛绒公仔。
Today was stuffing animal toys.

A　　很没趣?
Boring?

B　　对。
Yes.

A   那你做了多少个?

How many did you make?

B   没有算过,一、两百个吧

No idea. One hundred. Two hundred. It's not like you count.

A   你有见到小陈吗?

And did you see Chen?

Pause.

有见到他吗?

Did you see him?

B   早上见过他

In the morning I saw him.

A   下午呢?

What about in the afternoon?

Beat.

B   没有,下午没见到。

No, I didn't see him in the afternoon.

Pause.

A   你不是说你每天都坐在同一个地方吗?

I thought you sat in the same place every day?

B   是啊。

I do.

A   那他不是跟你一样吗?

And I thought he had to sit in the same place as well?

B   他是啊。

He does.

Pause.

A 有人占了他的位子?

Was someone in his seat?

B 也没有。

No.

Pause.

A 或许他换到其他地方去了。

Well maybe he moved.

Silence.

那是什么玩具?什么动物?

What were the toys? What animals?

B 不跟你聊了。

No more talking.

A 什么颜色?我喜欢想象不同的颜色,还有他们用的各种颜料和染料。

Or colours? I love thinking about that, all the different colours, the paints and dyes they must use.

B 你喜欢是你的事,不代表我也喜欢。

You like thinking about it. I don't want to.

A –

B 他们把他带走以后,我有去过他的工作台。

I went over to his workstation after they took him away.

Beat.

A 什么?

What?

B 他们把他带走以后,我有去过他的工作台。

I went over to his workstation after they took him away.

A 为什么?

Why?

B 他桌上有个未完成的玩具，像在瞪着我看，于是我过去把它的脸转到另一边。

He had a half-finished toy on it. I felt like it was looking at me. I went over and turned it away. Made it look at the wall.

A 那是什么玩具？

What toy was it?

B 好了，不跟你讲了。

No. No more now.

A 告诉我吧。

Please tell me.

B –

A 拜托。

Please.

B –

A 我只是想转移一下注意力。

不用老是胡思乱想。

So I can think about something else.

So I don't have to listen to myself.

Silence whilst they continue with the computer game.

我想小休一会儿。

I would like a break.

Pause.

我要休息。

I want a break.

Pause.

我要休息。

I want a break.

B 现在不是时候。
Well. You can't have one.

A 我要怒吼，直到筋疲力竭为止。
I want to scream. I want to scream until I'm sick.

Silence.

来跟我一起休息。
Have a break with me.

B 好吧。
Alright.

A –

B 喝杯热茶？
A cup of tea?

A –

B 吃个蛋挞，玩玩纸牌？
An egg tart and a game of cards?

A –

B 到花园去散个步？
Go for a walk in the garden?

A –

B 傻子。
Fool.

Silence.

A 小傅，过来一起休息。
Come Fu, have a break, a rest with me.

B –

A 我们大可停工。
We could stop.

B 你疯了。

You've gone mad.

A 我是认真的。

We can.

B –

A 我们可以停工。

We can stop.

B –

A 真的可以。

We could.

B 是你想休息,你自己停就好了。

Look. You want a break. You stop.

Silence.

A 要是我们一起停工五分钟,大可说网络故障了。

If we stop together for five minutes, we can say the network crashed.

B 这网络是不会故障的。

The network will not crash.

A 去年网络时好时坏,我们可以-

It was patchy last year we could –

B 去年没有什麽问题啊。

It wasn't patchy last year.

A 明明就有,是服务器出了问题。

It was, there were problems with the servers.

B 那是至少两年前的事了。

That was two years ago. Maybe more.

A   噢。

Oh.

Pause.

要是我们同时停工五分钟，我们可以说-

If we stopped for five minutes together, at the same time. If we do it together we can say –

B   老板说他回来要看到十万块黄金，现在他快要回来了。

Boss said he wanted to see a hundred thousand pieces of gold next time he comes in. He'll be in soon.

A   你怎么知道?

How do you know?

B   他总是很快回来。

He's always in soon.

A *whimpers, moans.*

A   我想休息。

I want to rest.

B   晚上睡觉就可以好好休息。

You rest when you sleep.

A   才不是呢。 就算趟在床上我也总是念念不忘，想着要去找黄金。 我的脑袋在睡觉 时还是继续在转，早上起来累个半死。

But I don't. This carries on in my sleep. I am my character, getting the gold. My brain carries on with the work when I'm asleep and then I wake up exhausted.

B   –

A   趁着现在人还清醒，还有能力控制就要停下来。

That's why I need to stop now. When I'm awake and in control and can feel it.

B   –

A   现在头脑清醒，有自制力，停了后才可以重拾感觉。

        I need to stop now so I can feel it. Whilst I'm awake and in control.

B   –

A   快来跟我一起休息。

        Come, rest with me.

B   继续工作吧。

        Do your work.

A   跟我小休一会儿。

        Take a break with me.

B   我不要。

        No.

A   要我们一起合作才能成事。

        It'll work if you do it with me.

B   这行不通的，我才不要。

        It won't. And I wouldn't.

A   我正需要你跟我合作，才不会闯祸。

        Exactly, if you do it with me, I won't get in trouble.

B   会给我添麻烦吗？

        Will I get in trouble?

A   保证不会。

        No. I promise.

B   –

        Pause.

A   我要小休。

        我要小休。

我要小休。
我要小休。
我要小休。
我要小休。
我要小休。
我要小休。
我要小休。
我要小休。
我要小休。
我要小休。
我要小休。
我要小休。
我要小休。
我要小休。
我要小休。
我要小休。
我要小休。
我要小休。
我要小休。
我要小休。
我要小休。
我要小休。
I want a break.
I want a break.
I want a break.
I want a break.
I want a break.

I want a break.

I want a break

I want a break.

I want a break.

I want a break.

I want a break.

I want a break.

I want a break.

I want a break.

I want a break

I want a break.

I want a break.

I want a break.

I want a break.

I want a break.

I want a break.

I want a break

I want a break.

B   好吧，好吧!

   Okay. Okay!

A   真的?

   Okay?

B   我们就稍微停工一下，这样行吗?

   We stop. For a really short time. Okay?

A   行。

   Okay.

They stop touching the keyboards. It feels unnatural, tense.

Long silence.

小傅，告诉我那些玩具是什么颜色的。

Tell me some of the colours of the toys Fu.

Pause.

B   全都是紫色的。

Purple. They were all purple.

Silence.

The machine whirrs and selects either Scene 10A or 10B.

9B. DETROIT. USA. 2016.

A sits down heavily near C.

Pause.

A   Hey

C   Yeah.

A   So, you see how I'm gonna give you this lift tomorrow?

C   Possible lift.

A   Possible lift yeah. So, you know, think you could do me a favour?

C   Okay. What?

A   I know it didn't go too well before but I was thinking, you take another look at the stuff I brought in? There's no obligation there just you might actually find something you want.

C   Alright, alright, just avoid the hard-sell shit, 'kay?

A   Okay. Just looking. No harm in looking.

A rummages in bag.

Okay. So. Well. But how about this?

Takes a wine charm out of their holdall. It is packaged in transparent plastic.

C   What the fuck is this?

A   It's a wine charm.

C   The fuck is a wine charm?

A   To make your wine, that bit more charming.

C   How?

A   It just wraps around the stem of your glass. It's decorative.

C   I don't even drink wine.

A   But if one day you did would you not want it to be charming?

C I mean this is what I mean. Lookit, you put two things together, not even things, two words, wine-charm, and you've got a product. Meanwhile, you've got us chumps making actual fucking machines, actual fucking quality automobiles and…

Pause.

I mean. Look at my hands. I ruined my hand making these cars man and now, you know, my lungs…

A I know.

C Yeah? And you know what the doctor said to me when I went in?

A Naw, what he say?

C He says 'You smoke?' Said 'Nope, never have.'

And he says well you've been very unlucky then.

I was like, thanks doc.

And he says 'Where do you work?'

I said the plant up on Madison.

He said you wear a mask?

I said no, don't need to, I don't work in the spray shop.

And he just looks at me.

Pause.

A What you saying?

C I'm just saying who knows what we're working in? Particles and shit floating around. And do they care? No. Not one of 'em. Not the company. Not the unions. Nobody cares. None.

A That's fucked up.

C Mm.

Pause.

Man, they shouldn't have any let this happen. Any of it.

A   What do you mean?

C   This used to be a great country. A great country. They shouldn'ta let it happen.

A   Who's they? And even if there is one, they don't give a shit where the cars are made, they just want the profit / they don't care

C   Well they should!

A   I don't believe in shoulds. I believe in what is –

C   Fuck you.

   Pause.

   Let me see that.

   A *tosses it over.* C *looks at it.*

   So this is actually new, not nearly new?

A   My brother couldn't make it out for Thanksgiving. It's unopened.

   Pause.

C   It's disgusting.

A   It's different, doesn't mean it's disgusting.

C   No, I mean the whole fucking set-up.

A   Well, I can agree with you on that one.

   Pause.

C   And how much you want for it?

A   Five dollars.

C   What's this design?

A   It's a cat. You're holding it upside down.

C   Oh yeah.

   Looks at it properly.

   Weird fucking cat.

A   –

C You ever think about where this came from?

A –

C What the person looks like? How much they got paid?

Pause.

Can tell you one thing, it sure as hell wasn't in America.

A No I paid two dollars for it so it definitely wasn't America.

C Two dollars?

Beat.

A Yeah.

C And you want five from me?

Pause.

A Well that was a starting. Guide price.

C A guide price?

A –

C Fuck you.

A –

C Fuck! You!

A –

C This is what I mean, no, unity. Whatseover. No unity!

A Okay. Okay.

C No. No! Hours been cut, wages been cut and my co-worker of what? Fifteen years? Wants to make a three-dollar profit off me for a TAWDRY PIECE OF EAST ASIAN SHIT!

C rips the package apart, a note slithers out.

C calms themself down.

Pause.

A has seen the note, picks it up and walks away. Reads it.

Pause.

C is calmer now and begins to pay attention.

What's that? The receipt? You gonna take it back now you can't make a fucking profit –

- A No it's a note.
- C What?
- A It's a written note.
- C From where?
- A Inside the thing.
- C Oh.

 Oh, I heard about stuff like that, what's it say?

 A reads it aloud.

- A 'One day all our future will the same.'

 Beat.

- C What's that?
- A 'One day all our future will the same.'

 C chuckles, then laughs, laughs uproariously which then turns into a nasty cough. Gathers themself.

- C Oh shit. Fuck me.

 C catches their breath.

 The machine whirrs and selects either Scene 10A or 10B.

10A. GUAYAQUIL. ECUADOR. 1992.

C *and* A *are looking at each other.*

C *is holding an orange balloon.* A *is holding forty-nine balloons of differing colours.*

B *arrives.*

B   No haga eso.

           You don't do that.

A   ¿Mande?

           What?

B   Hey! que hace? No le dará un globo a mi guagua!

           I'm not happy. You do not give a balloon to a child.

A   Ella me lo pidió.

           She reached her hand out.

B   Tiene cinco años.

           She's five.

A   Cuando mis guaguas tenían cinco años no pedían globos en la calle.

           When my children were five they would not have reached their hand out.

           Pause.

           Los guaguas saben. Ella sabe quién soy. / Simón, ella sabe lo que vendo. Sabe que no está chiro y puede pagarlo.

           Children know. She knows who I am. / She knows what I sell. She knows you can afford it.

B   El vendedor de globos.

           The balloon seller.

           Beat.

A   Usted me compra globos casi todos los sábados y siempre ha sido chévere conmigo.

	You've bought balloons before. Every Saturday, near enough. You've always been pleasant before.
B	Sí, pero siempre he de pagarle antes de que le dé el globo a mi niña. Hoy le dió un globo a mi bebé para asegurar que le pague.
	Yes but previously you have taken my money in order that I may give my child a balloon.
	Today you gave my child a balloon so you could take my money.
A	Verá mi ñaño, ella corrió hacia mí sonriendo, y me pidió el globo naranja, así que…
	She ran up to me smiling, hands out, asking for the orange one so…
B	¿Se lo dió?
	You gave it to her?
A	Sí.
	Yes.
B	Así no más
	Just like that
A	Sí.
	Yes.
B	Usted vende globos. Seguramente la mayoría de los peques corren aquí, felices a pedirle un globo
	You sell balloons. Surely most kids run up to you with excited eyes and their hands outstretched?
A	–
B	¿Aprenderá que no puede darle globos a todos los peques que se acerquen?
	You haven't learned to fight that urge yet?
A	¿Comprará un globo?
	Were you going to buy a balloon?

B	–
A	¿Va a comprar un globo, señor?
	Were you going to buy a balloon sir?
B	¿Que cuesta el globo?
	How much is a balloon?
A	¿Mande?
	What?
B	¿Que cuesta el globo?
	How much is a balloon?
A	Usted sabe ñaño.
	You know how much.
B	No, para usted, ¿cuánto paga por los globos?
	No, for you, how much do you pay for the balloons?
	Pause.
	Puede decirme.
	You can tell me.
	Pause.
	¿Gana mucho?
	Do you make much?
A	No señor, no gano mucho.
	No, sir, I do not make much.
B	No gana mucho.
	You do not make much.
A	No señor, no gano mucho.
	No sir, I do not make much.
B	¿Con cuántos globos inicias el día?
	How many balloons do you start the day with?

A   Cincuenta Ñaño.

Fifty.

B   ¿Y Cuántos globos tiene ahí?

And how many do you have now?

A   Cuarenta y nueve.

Forty-nine.

B   No ha vendido nada.

No sales.

A   Es temprano.

It's early.

B   ¿Por qué empieza con cincuenta? ¿Es eso lo que puede pagar?

Why do you start with fifty? Is that how much you can afford?

A   No, puedo permitirme más

No I can afford more.

B   ¿No vende más de cincuenta al día?

You don't sell more than fifty a day?

A   Hay cincuenta estrellas de la bandera de Estados Unidos.

There are fifty stars on the flag of the United States of America.

B   Ajá.

Aha.

A   Mis guaguas quieren estudiar allí.

My boys want to study there.

B   ¿Cómo harán?

How will they manage that?

A   Chuta! No sé.

No idea.

B   Niños.

Kids.

A   Niños.

Kids.

B   (*To* C.) Devuélvelo.

(*To* C.) Return it.

C begins to wail, big fat tears.

¡DEVUÉLVELO!

RETURN IT!

C hands the balloon back to A.

Silence.

Okay. ¿Cuál quiere?

Okay. Which one?

C   El naranja.

The orange one.

B   ¿Mande?

I can't hear you.

C   El naranja.

The orange one.

B   Le dirás al señor.

Now say it to him.

Beat.

C   ¿Me da el naranja, por favor?

Can I have the orange one please?

A   Sí, por supuesto, mija.

Yes of course mija.

C   Gracias.

Thank you.

A   Ya mija.

It's nothing.

B   ¿Qué cuesta?

How much?

A   Cincuenta centavos.

Fifty centavos.

B *hands over a note.* A *just looks at it, surprised.*

¿No tiene suelto?

Do you want lots of change?

B   No, quédeselo.

No.

A   Oh. Gracias. Gracias Ñaño.

Oh. Thank you. Thank you.

B   No es nada. Chao.

It's nothing. Bye.

A   Pase bien.

Have a good day.

B   Pase bien.

Have a good day.

B *and* C *move away. After a few steps* B *stops and turns.*

Amigo.

Friend.

A   ¿Mande?

Yes?

B	Su cambio.
	The money.
A	Sí.
	Yes.
B	No es un regalo mijo. Es un pago.
	It's not a gift. It's a payment.

Pause.

Los dejarás ir.

Let go.

Silence.

A *lets go of all their balloons, they float into the sky.*

Vamos, mija.

Come on mija.

B *and* C *turn and leave.*

The next scene is Scene 11.

10B. HERTFORDSHIRE. ENGLAND. 2017.

C and B are six-year-olds. They watch as A sweeps up the remains of the plate that has / hasn't been smashed. C tugs B and motions to follow them into another space, C's bedroom. A leaves.

Silence.

B   I'm really sorry about the plate.

C   –

B   I thought your mum was going to shout.

C   No she doesn't really shout. She just goes quiet and still.

B   It's more scary than shouting I think.

    C nods.

    Beat.

    I like your room.

C   It's cool isn't it? Orange.

    B admires the room.

    You wanna see my piggy bank.

B   Your what?

C   Well it's a money box really.

B   What's that?

C   For my money.

B   Is it a toy?

C   No.

B   Why's it good then?

C   Well it stores my money.

B   Bit boring.

C   Money isn't boring.

B   –

C   This lets me save up.

B	Okay.
C	It's good to have more money.
B	Okay.
C	Because more money will get you more things.
B	Like what?
C	Whatever I want.
B	What d'you want?
C	I don't know. But do you want to know how much I've got?
B	How much?
C	Seventy pounds.
B	Wow. I think I've got like two pounds at home.
C	Two pounds?
B	Yeah. A two-pound coin.
C	Who gave you that?
B	Found it.
C	Where?
B	In my living room.
C	–
B	What you going to spend it on? You could get a lightsaber!
C	I do not want a lightsaber.
B	–
C	You wanna see something really cool though?
B	Yeah.

C *pulls a fifty-pound note out of the piggy bank.*

What's that?

C	Fifty-pound note.

112   THE LEGEND OF NED LUDD

B   –

C   My dad gave me twenty pounds and I said is there anything more than a twenty-pound note and he said fifty pounds and I said can I have that and he said maybe, and the next time I saw him he gave this to me. He said a lot of shops won't even take it because they won't actually believe it's real, because it's so much money.

B   If the shops won't take it what's the point of it?

C   It's a fifty-pound note.

Pause. C toys with the note.

Do you want it?

B *shrugs*.

Would you like it?

B   No.

C   You can't have it.

B   Okay.

C   But you do want it.

B   I don't really care.

C   You do want it.

B   No. I don't really care.

C   –

B   –

C   Think of all the things you could buy with it.

B   Don't really want anything. Except maybe like an ice cream or something.

C   So you do want this then.

B   I can buy an ice cream with my two pounds at home.

C   But you could buy like twenty-seven ice creams with this.

B   I don't want that many ice creams I'd get a brain freeze.

C   Oh. I hate brain freeze.

B   I know like when you drink a slushie and you're like, this is nice this is nice this is nice oooooowwwwwww!

They laugh.

C   But then you can't not drink it.

B   No. It's too good.

C   I've got fifty pounds. And then a twenty. Seventy pounds.

Pause.

I can't really give you the fifty pounds but I can give you the twenty.

B   Really?

C   Yeah.

B   Wow. / Thanks.

C   But you have to do something for it?

B   Like what?

C   Like… dares.

B   I like dares.

C   Mmmm.

I dare you to eat a worm.

B   Where's a worm?

C   Ummm.

Take your socks off.

B *does so.*

Smell it.

B *does so.*

What does it smell of?

B   Cheese on toast.

They laugh.

C   Lick it.

B   Ewww.

B does it, quickly.

C   Does it taste of cheese on toast?

B   No, tastes of salt.

C   Take your trousers off.

B   What?

C   Take your trousers off.

B   Why?

C   'Sfunny.

B does so.

Now do a little dance.

B does so. Stops.

More.

B   This is boring, I feel stupid.

C   Twenty pounds… you could buy a lightsaber.

B dances for a long time, until it feels uncomfortable.

B   I'm tired.

C   Kneel down.

B does so.

B goes over, turns around.

Kiss my bum.

B considers. Gives a quick peck.

C turns around.

Put your head here.

C pushes B's head into their crotch, it's not sexual but has clearly been copied from something that is.

Don't laugh.

B   What?

C   Stop laughing.

Beat.

Look at me.

They make eye contact and hold it.

Pause.

Tell me I'm big.

B   What?

C   Tell me I'm big.

B   You're big.

C   Again.

B   You're big.

Silence.

C scutters off, giggling.

C   Okay. You've passed all the dares.

Hands over the twenty-pound note.

Here you go. It's yours now then.

B   Thanks.

Pause.

C   Be happy! It's twenty pounds!

B   Yeah.

C   Think of all the things you could buy?

You can get a lightsaber.

Silence.

Do you want to play that the floor is lava?

Silence.

The next scene is Scene 11.

11. NOTTINGHAM. ENGLAND. 1816.

C and B work.

They are digging a hole.

It is the size of a small grave.

It is real work.

They are tired.

They are hungry.

We watch them work.

The heavens open.

They pay no attention.

They continue to work as it pisses down.

If anything they work harder, faster.

As if possessed.

It is manic.

It is horrible.

The lights fade as we leave them with their work.

The machine whirrs and selects either Scene 12A or 12B.

12A. HERE. NOW.

An actor, or combination of actors, recites the below.

You probably don't want to think about all the ways that work is worked.

You probably don't want to think of all the various ways.

That right now.

Work is being worked.

The millions of unseen cogs

Of corked and coiled springs

Of rotary blades.

And jackhammers.

The gaskets, pistons and crankshafts.

The belt fans and cylinders,

A million screws meeting a million bolts.

How many tonnes of coolant churning over how many heads right now?

At this very moment

How many swear words

Uttered in how many languages

As how many fingers

Mutely press control alt delete.

How many lonely walks to jammed-up printer trays?

How many things sold?

How many things bought?

How many people saying

We heard you were in an accident that wasn't your fault?

Beat.

How many needles? How many blisters?

How many feel like they're dropping dead and how many dead drops?

How many sweat shops?

How much work and aspects of work do we not only not want to think about but actually want to actively forget.

The sluices.

The sounds of pain

The cellophane

The contrails,

Entrails

Passive-aggressive emails.

The details.

The brushstrokes broad.

The boring board meetings where you're already bored.

The balance between life and what you can afford.

The lack of pause.

The lack of grace.

Beat.

The empty race

The Polyfilla to fill the space

The things to focus on to take that place.

Bent backs,

Those that can't snap back.

Or slap back

The roads, the tyres.

All the things on fire,

The bottles of wine.

The turpentine.

The counterpoints, the counterweights,

The contingencies to counter fate.

The ports the docks

The drowsily snatched and mismatched socks

The navy the army

Those that could

But would never harm me

The broken jokes that still get laughs.

The complaints slips,

The container ships

The air miles.

The mandatory smiles.

The bloodied fingers.

The stumps.

The rat poison.

The pumps.

The tea runs.

The livestock.

The shares.

The nets.

The thrashing.

The vaguely worded threats,

Overflowing inboxes filling out our screens.

The slaughterhouses insulated blocking out our screams

The things the machines can't do.

Won't do.

The glue.

The pain.

The prayers for rain.

The oil slicks

How many fried chips?

How many people going how much will people admire this?

At this moment now.

How many implements busting into the earth right now.

How many shovels and hoes and rakes and spades?

How many hotel bedspreads made.

Ripping into the soil.

The polythene bags.

The lags.

The zooms.

The gravestones,

The tombs.

The marvel of work in the marblework.

Floors wet with blood.

Floors wet with love.

The mop that isn't clean enough.

The leaching,

The bleaching.

Networks to guesswork

Merchandise and fertiliser

The strain

The baby oil

The broken soil.

Lights fade out.

The machine whirrs and selects either Scene 13A or 13B.

12B. HERE. THEN.

An actor, or combination of actors, recites the below.

(*There is reference here to actual names of the technicians who were sub-stage but this can be swapped for someone else who is offstage, the deputy stage manager for instance.*)

Sometimes

It is useful

Or, more like, instructive

To think about the foundations

Or maybe not so much the foundations

But like just what sits beneath

The surface

This surface

Like

Literally, at this very moment

There are people sub-stage,

Kaila and Jack

Are underneath us right now

Working their arses off

Unseen

Hauling wardrobes onto pallets

Scrabbling and sweating around in the dark underneath

Quietly swearing and struggling

So that things can appear

Here before us

And we can pretend

That it's magic.

Beat.

They won't get a bow

No they won't get a bow

A lot of people won't get a bow.

A lot of people who are sweating and scrabbling in the dark underneath

Carrying burdens in places that we forgot

Will not get a bow

Within the building

And beyond.

And beneath

Because

Because beneath Kaila and Jack

Yes beneath them

Beneath their shoes

There are others

Other bodies

Hands

Limbs

And layers

And levels

And substrates

And stratas

Of people who scrabbled

And toiled

And grafted

And died

Beneath us

In the selfsame dirt.

People who lay

Their shovels and their bones

At the foot of our cathedrals

In our foundations

The actual foundations

Of everything that comes after

And even if we don't acknowledge them

And their history

Don't look them full in the face

Those people

Are still there

They still sit

Watching us now

They can't not

Because their spit

Is in our mortar

Their blood is in the bricks

Of all our buildings,

Our tunnels,

Our towers.

The sweat and marrow of

The low-paid

Underpaid

The people who were never paid

They sit here

Restless

Or restful

Their bones prop up our buildings

English bones

Ghanaian bones

Irish bones

Jamaican bones

Chinese bones

Norwegian bones

Scottish bones

German bones

Polish bones

Welsh bones

Human bones

Human bones

Human bones

Lights fade out.

The machine whirrs and selects either Scene 13A or 13B.

13A. GUWAHATI. INDIA. 2023.

In the darkness we hear the following with a translation in English flashing up as a projection.

The bleep of a voicemail message.

हैलो मम्मी।

मैं बोल रही हूँ।

कोई घबराने की जरूरत नहीं है, कोई अर्जेंट बात नहीं है, मैं ठीक हूँ और मेरे को पता है कि आप काम पर हो।

मैं तो फोन कर रही थी था इसलिए कि उम्म... समझ गई।

मुझे लगा मुझे एक हफ्ता रुकना पड़ेगा, या वो लोग मेरे को फोन करेंगे, पर उन लोगों ने आखिर में बस ये बोला कि मुझे मिल गई है।

और मम्मी मैं बहुत नर्वस थी। थोड़ा कांप भी रही थी। मुझे लगा वो लोग भी मेरी घबराहट समझ रहे थे।

खैर, मेरे को पता है कि ये कोई बहुत बड़ी चीज नहीं है, बस एक छोटी, ...बस एक नौकरी है पर मैं बहुत खुश हूँ।

तो, बस आपको यही बताना था, पता है आप बिजी हो, काम पर हो, आज रात को मिलती हूँ आपसे।

बस आपको बताना था।

क्योंकि मैं बहुत खुश हूँ। आई लव यू।

आज रात को मिलती हूँ।

बाय।

***

Hello Mummy.

It's me.

No need to panic or anything, it's not an emergency, and I'm okay I know you're working.

I'm just ringing because umm… I got it.

I thought I'd have to wait for a week, or they'd ring me or, but they just told me at the end that I'd got it.

And I was so nervous Mum. I was even shaking a little bit. I felt like they could see it.

So, anyway, I know it's not a big thing, it's just a small... it's just a job but I'm so happy.

So happy.

So I just wanted to tell you, I know you're busy, I know you're working, I'll see you tonight.

I just wanted to tell you.

Because I'm excited. I love you.

See you tonight.

Bye.

Lights up.

13B. SABRATHA. LIBYA. 2020.

In the darkness we hear the following voice message with the English translation flashing up as a projection.

The bleep of a voicemail message.

Salut Maman,

Le moteur est tombé en panne.

Il faut qu'un certain nombre de choses aillent mal avant que les choses aillent bien.

Mais il y a des choses qui brillent sur la côte.

Tu sais ce que c'est, maman.

L'espoir.

L'espoir.

Aie la foi.

Je t'aime Maman.

Je t'enverrai bientôt un peu d'argent

***

Hello Maman,

The engine failed.

A certain amount of things have to go wrong before things go right.

But there are glinting things on the coast.

You know what it is Maman.

Hope.

Hope.

Have faith.

I love you Maman.

I will send you some money soon.

Lights up.

14. THE CAST

The cast are stood in the positions they were in during Scene 1. Again, there is room here to improvise off these lines and connect with the audience.

A   Hello

C   Hi again.

B   Hello. We're near the end now.

C   And you know what a job can be like

A   Sometimes your work feels heavy and impossible doesn't it?

B   And sometimes it feels light

A   Some days it just glides along

C   And other days, it's just bloody hard graft.

A   But we just wanted to stop, for a second, and say thank you, for watching us, work

B   And, also, for working quite hard yourself

C   Because there's a lot going on isn't there?

Beat.

A   There is.

B   And finally can I just say if anyone is sat there going 'hang on, have I missed out on some brilliant scenes?' … yeah you have.

Beat.

A   So, this, is the penultimate scene in the play.

C   And the next one is a scene that we do in every performance

B   The play might be flexible but it ends the same way every night

C   Some stories are open

FOURTEEN 129

A   Some stories are closed.

B   Some stories have endings that are inevitable

C   And this one does.

15. NOTTINGHAM. ENGLAND. 1816.

C enters with a plate. Identical to the one in Scene 4B.

C	Ey up duck.
B	Ey up.
C	–
B	What's that for then?
C	Don't even begin.
B	What? You can't wander round town carrying plate and think folk'll not say oat.
C	–
B	You haven't bought it.
C	No.
B	–
C	I finished the piecework for Rodgers. And he said he didn't have any money coz a shipment hadn't come in from London and all he could give me was this.
B	A plate. Is he taking the piss? We're going hungry and he gives you a plate.
	Beat.
C	Said it's worth more than me wages.
B	If it was he wouldn't give it ya.
C	I know.
B	What did you say?
C	I said
B	Did you say it's in the charter / that he can't pay you in goods or plates or crockery or any other
C	I said it's in the charter
	I said it's in the charter.
B	And what say him to that
C	Said he knows that but it's this or nowt.

B   You didn't stand up to him.

C   I said to him I don't want a plate, I want me fucking dinner.

         Silence.

         A *enters carrying a large rifle.*

A   Ey up.

C   Ey up.

B   Ey up.

A   Not working then?

         Pause.

B   Work without pay isn't work.

A   You not being paid?

B   Not enough.

A   –

B   See you're working.

A   That's right.

C   How goes it?

A   Fine.

B   Proud of yourself are yer?

A   You what?

B   Proud of yourself?

A   Maybe I am.

B   Walking round with a rifle in your finery.

A   –

B   Like Billy Big Bollocks himself.

A   –

B   You look good.

A   Thank you.

B	Shot anyone yet?
A	No.
B	Give it time.
C	When did you sign up?
A	Month ago.
C	Thought I hadn't seen yer but I didn't think it would be that.

Pause.

B	I remember, when you were seven, you crying when our Bertie skinned a rabbit.
	–
	Do you remember that?
A	Can't say I do.
B	I do. Can you?
C	–
B	Walking round with a gun and yet you bawled your eyes out when a rabbit died.
A	I'm sure the rabbit hadn't done anything wrong.
B	Oh. Fuck me. Wrongdoers, is that right?
A	–
B	Where do we start? What's a wrongdoer?
A	–
B	What's a wrongdoer?

Those who were promised work and were given none.

Those who were stupid enough to believe the guarantees that were sold to them.

Those who thought their children would eat the same, if not more.

Maybe those are the wrongdoers.

	Or maybe, it's those who build their wealth upon the misery of others
	Those who go back on their word and have the temerity to look the other way
	Or is it simply those who betray their kith and their kin?

A   –

C   How's your dad?

A   He's not well.

B   Least he's alive.

A   –

B   Is he proud of you?

A   –

B   Is he proud of you?

A   –

C   He doesn't know does he?

Beat.

A   He knows that I bring him bread and meat.

B   Bread and meat.

A   –

B   I wish my girls had lived long enough to bring me bread and meat when I be sick.

Silence.

    What's your job?

A   I'm soldier.

B   Yes but what's your job?

A   I serve His Majesty –

B   Yes but what's your job? What do you need to do to make your boss happy?

A   I'm here to kill Ned Ludd and his followers.

B Oh. Sounds easy.

C Easy enough.

   B *and* C *laugh*.

   You hunt ghosts lad.

B Better off catching farts.

   C *and* B *laugh*.

   Do you believe in him?

A Yes.

B You think he's real?

A Yes. Do you?

B Oh I know he's real.

C John.

B What?

Pause.

A How do you know he's real?

Beat.

B Because so many people believe in him.

A –

B And if enough people believe in something then it's real isn't it?

A –

B Like money. Or god. Or honour.

Pause.

B And also, someone must be writing those letters.

C John.

B What?

Pause.

B   Did you see the one tacked up by town hall?

A   Yes.

B   To the Gentlemen Hosiers of Nottingham and surrounding areas in the year of our Lord 1816. Our lords and betters, we humbly appeal to you in this time of calamity and distress;

A   Off by heart?

B   Off by heart.

A   You think that's clever?

B   –

A   Do you think that's clever?

B   It's quite clever, it's not the cleverest thing I've done.

C   / John

A   What the cleverest thing you've done?

B   That would be telling.

A   Go on.

C   John.

B   You wouldn't believe it if you knew.

C   John.

A   Try me.

B   The cleverest thing I've done is…

A   –

C   –

B   I.

         Found a way out.

         Beat.

         B *laughs. It is an odd laugh.*

A   What does he mean?

C   I don't know. He's not well.

B   Would you like to know who wrote those letters?

    Beat.

A   You're teasing me.

C   John.

B   You'd rather not know. That's quite wise. If you do
    find Ludd then there's nowt left to search for. And you
    haven't got a job any more.
    You think your trade's safe and then, like that, it's gone.
    They say work harder, strive harder.
    The machine strives for nothing.
    The loom does the work twice as fast and half as well.
    And they'll settle for that. They'll settle for that.
    They told us our wages couldn't be raised as the work
    Would up and go to France.
    So we bit our tongue and bided our time
    Waited for the trade to rise,
    We waited, like a stranded rotting whaler,
    Begging for the tide to rise us up and carry us into
    fairer waters
    But alas we're in Nottingham. We'll never see the tide.
    And nothing and no one is coming to save us.
    Except Ned Ludd.

C   John.

    Pause.

B   You know who Ludd is don't you lad?

C   John!

B   It'll all be well. We're on our way.

    Beat.

    You know who Ludd is don't you lad?

    Beat.

A   Who is he?

    Beat.

B	He is. All of us.
	Silence.
	So if you want to tell the captain that you've killed Ludd.
A	–
B	Here he is.
C	John.
	Perfect silence.
A	If you think I am scared, I am not scared.
B	You are scared. As you should be. This is the day you find out whether you're a little child playing dress up, or a man.
A	–
B	And are you going to tell the captain that you had Ned Ludd in your grasp and you just let him slip away?
C	John. Stop jesting with him now.
A	–
B	I can't fight. I can't work. I can't go to church because I can't walk past me girls.
	And I'm too scared of hell to take my own life.
	No courage
	But I can write.
	Me mum taught me.
	Beat.
	Would you like to know who wrote those letters?
A	–
C	–
B	I did.
	It were me.

A	I am going to shoot you, if you give me / cause
B	No you're not, you're just a boy, a colt, you couldn't shoot a fucking rabbit.
A	–
B	It were me.

    Me

    It were me.

    But then

    There were others

    There were those that

    Watched

    Those that bore witness

    Hundreds

    Thousands

    The Chinese man with bleeding fingers and a stolen pen.

    The factory worker in Detroit with a cough and nowt to make.

    The Cameroonian woman thousands of miles from home

    Untold others

    Uncountable others

    But I wrote them.

    Me

    Me

    Me

A	–
B	And my name is

    Ned Ludd.

General

Lord

Ned

Ludd.

Ned Ludd.

I

am

Ned

Ludd.

General, Lord, Ned, Ludd.

/ Me

A   This is a / warning –

B   Shoot me and I'll live forever.

Do not shoot me and watch as I

And my followers

Tear your world apart.

Me.

General

Lord

Ned

Ludd

I am

Ned Ludd.

I am.

I am

Ned Ludd.

Ned Ludd.

Ned Ludd.

Ned Ludd. Ned Ludd. Ned Ludd. Ned Ludd. Ned Ludd. Ned Ludd. Ned Ludd. Ned Ludd. Ned Ludd. Ned Ludd.

I AM NED LUUUUUUUUUUUU–

A *shoots* B.

It blows a large hole in B*'s stomach.*

Shock and silence.

B *silently writhes in their own blood.* C *sinks beside* B *to help but there is no help to be had.*

Just the sound of C *and* A *breathing.*

Snowflakes begin to drift down from the sky.

They flutter slowly down to the floor as A *and* C *watch.*

They look up as the snow falls.

End.

LIVERPOOL everyman & PLAYHOUSE

At the Everyman and Playhouse, we believe that theatre inspires creative lives. We bring artists, audiences and our communities together in a celebration of what great theatre can achieve.

With two exceptional Liverpool venues united by our mission to entertain and inspire, we create unforgettable experiences built from innovation, talent and a passion for social change.

Whether you visit us at the Everyman or the Playhouse, see our work online or out in the community, we promise you an exhilarating theatrical adventure and a whole new way of looking at the world.

We are a registered charity (1081229) and gratefully acknowledge the continued support of Arts Council England, Liverpool City Council, our donors, patrons, partners and our audiences.

To find out how you can support us, please visit everymanplayhouse.com/support-us.

Chief Executive:
Mark Da Vanzo

Trustees:
Andrea Nixon (Chair), Paul Bibby, James Bierman, Helen Blakeman, Natasha Bucknor, Amy Causley, Mike Clarke, Paul Evans, Jill Jones, Camilla Mankabady, Caroline Sanger-Davies, Tony Smith

Thank you to all Everyman & Playhouse staff

 everymanplayhouse.com   0151 709 4776

 @LivEveryPlay    @everymanplayhouse    @LivEveryPlay

www.nickhernbooks.co.uk

facebook.com/nickhernbooks

twitter.com/nickhernbooks